In Memory of

Ruth Garrison Scurlock

Mary and John Gray Library
Lamar University

PAISANO BOOKS

Number Three

WILSON M. HUDSON, *Editor*

PAISANO BOOKS *are a series brought out at irregular intervals by the Texas Folklore Society in addition to its annual volume. They are published by the Encino Press and may be ordered from the publisher or the Society.*

Aunt Puss & Others

Aunt Puss & Others

Old Days in the Piney Woods

by EMMA WILSON EMERY

1969 : THE ENCINO PRESS : *Austin*

TO MY FAMILY
Because they didn't howl when I dragged our skeletons out into the open

Photographs of East Texas scenes courtesy Frances Abernethy
Family photographs provided by the author

© 1969 : TEXAS FOLKLORE SOCIETY : Austin
Printed in the United States of America

Foreword

IF THE CONTINUITY of this story seems faulty and the narrative broken by the sudden intrusion of unrelated phrases, please know it is because a dreamer is taking dictation from the subconscious, catching incidents at random as they rise through the pale mist of memory.

If you see contradictory statements, be generous. Seventy-five years is a long space of time in a woman's life, and when it covers the transitory period from crinolined modesty to streamlined sophistication one should be forgiven if one's viewpoint turns a somersault and takes root on the other side of the fence.

Except for my mother and father, I shall have little to say about my immediate family. It is a large and interesting family but modest, a family that would not like any eye or remark turned in its direction as a result of being included in this book.

Men's life stories have been told in various ways since papyrus and quill gave a medium through which their dreams could be recorded. This is just another story by another dreamer who hopes to paint a word picture so simple in truth that it will warm the hearts of those who like to turn back the pages of time and gaze into yesteryears.

The people concerned in the story are real people who lived in East Texas before the turn of the century. Among them there were few dual personalities. They lived their lives by a simple pattern which had been handed down to them by their ancestors. For many years their families made up an unbroken circle, but eventually some of them spilled over into the state of Louisiana. One of these was my father, David Henry Wilson.

When my great-grandfather, William M. Wilson, got ready to settle in the Republic of Texas in 1837, he drew in his reins and said, "Whoa, there, Nick, whoa, Nancy," then looked about and surveyed his worldly possessions, which consisted of two lean mules and a covered wagon. The wagon contained a few groceries, a box of chipped crockery and battered tinware, two rawhide-bottom chairs, some bedding, and a wife who was expecting a baby any minute.

There was not a soul within three miles of where he stopped. But there was a stream of cool, clear water gushing out of a nearby hillside, and that was good enough for Mr. Wilson.

Darkness was settling over the forest when Will Wilson crawled from his wagon seat and rubbed the tired muscles of his legs. Then he built a fire and soon his wife Sallie had their meager supper ready. After they had eaten, Will looked at the bright stars overhead, yawned, stretched his long arms upward and said, "Sallie, I bet you can hear Almighty God's still, small voice out here without even listenin'." "Yes, I bet you can," Sallie agreed. "I like it," Will said. "Think I'll settle here." Taking a deep, easy breath, he continued, "Just look at the stars up there a-twinklin'." He chuckled, "Yes, reckon I'll settle right here." Sallie, who sat on the other chair, looked up and said, "Will, that sounds good." So right then and there was founded, not far from the Neches River in what was later to become the fabulous state of Texas, the little town of Spurger where my forebears lived out their long and useful lives.

EMMA WILSON EMERY

Shreveport, Louisiana
September 23, 1967

Contents

Foreword	vii
Aunt Puss	3
Uncle Christopher Columbus Hooks	9
Aunt Puss Goes Visiting	11
Aunt Puss at the Exercises	13
Aunt Puss Goes Dancing	13
Aunt Puss's Chickens	15
Aunt Puss and Religion	16
Aunt Puss Gets Lost	24
Henry Wilson Runs off with Eula Gilmore	29
Uncle Faith	26
The Syrian Peddler-Woman	32
The Dawsons	33
Rebecca Sheffield Hooks	36
Uncle Noah	41
Aunt Chlo and Uncle Bill	42
Papa	43
Jewel	45
Mama	46
Ellie	49
Pappy	51
Aunt Sue and Uncle Bob	56

Miss Kate Sawyer	59
Morogan's Terrible Men	62
Macbeth *in Beaumont*	65
The Sawmill Changes Hands	67
We Move to Louisiana	70
I Fall in Love	72
Joe's Horseless Carriage	75
Papa Plants His Family in the Wilderness	76
My Fortune in Boyce	79
I Try Teaching	82
Mama and the Burglars	86
More About Papa	90
Papa's Baths	91
Papa and Music	94
Good-Bye, Aunt Puss	95

Aunt Puss & Others

Aunt Puss and Uncle Lum

Aunt Puss

IN 1890, Aunt Puss Hooks, Spurger's outstanding citizen, was not known beyond the boundaries of Tyler County, Texas. She never saw the halls of Congress nor went shopping on Fifth Avenue, but she represented a way of life as it was lived in her day and a type of people who were among the unsung builders of our nation. Belonging to a generation that had its advent immediately following the conflict between our states, she was one of the children who had to go to the cottonfield instead of the schoolhouse.

Although Aunt Puss had no formal education, she possessed its equivalent in her innate nobility of character, understanding of nature in all its forms, and the capacity for love of God and her fellow man that made her a shining light to those who shared the simple joys and sorrows of her narrow world. She was not a retiring, subdued woman as were most other women in the piney woods. Hers was a positive personality, the blending of a fighting spirit with an unselfish, gentle nature that filled her critics with awe and her friends with love and admiration. And, despite her pious leanings, Aunt Puss could let go a mild cuss-word when greatly agitated.

Aunt Puss was medium tall, average in weight, and ruggedly built. She moved with the grace of a creature of the wilds. She talked as rapidly as she walked, and one had to be closely attentive to catch her racing words and build them into sentences. She seldom changed her mind. Once she'd said something, that was her opinion, and final! In any unpleasant situation the set of her jaw said more than any word she could have spoken. To me, as a child, Aunt Puss was a three ring circus all by herself. I loved her dearly and I believe you will enjoy knowing this lovable, backwoods woman.

At the age of sixteen Aunt Puss was already a potent force for law and order in the little community where she was born and lived out her life, in Spurger, my great-grandfather's little town that lay in the bend of Beech Creek. One day after the town gossip spread the story that Aunt Puss's favorite cousin had been seen having a high-heeled time in the "Square Moon," Spurger's only barroom, she shouldered her musket and walked into the place to give the proprietor a piece of her mind.

"Now, see here, Mr. Sistrunk, I'm warnin' you, if I ever hear tell any more of my kinfolks have been seen in this devil's roost, I'll blow it so full of holes it won't hold water, much less'n whiskey." Knowing my future aunt to be a woman of her word, and for other reasons known only to himself, the owner of the saloon closed its doors and a few days later he opened up for business under a new name near Woodville, a town thirty miles north of Spurger. When Aunt Puss heard this she said, "Thank the Lord for that. The Square Moon!" she muttered disgustedly. "I reckon the moon does look square to them that stumble out of there with their bellies full and their pockets empty."

Just how Aunt Puss was able to lead my great-uncle Christopher Columbus Hooks, a lover of Shakespeare, to the marriage altar was a mystery to all who knew them. Some thought it was her sparkling black eyes that propelled him, but others said it was the ease and grace with which she could dismount her horse while he was still in a trot that swept Uncle Lum into matrimony.

Uncle Lum was several years older than Spurger's number one vigilante. Before his marriage he never openly kept company with her because he didn't want his friends to start talking about wedding bells; but word got around that he'd been seen entering her front gate as late as seven o'clock at night. It wasn't long before her father, Mr. Utah Pettigo, stood up one morning after church service and announced: "All friends and members of this congregation will be welcome here next Sunday morning at ten o'clock to see my daughter Puss wedded to Mr. Christopher Columbus Hooks." He hesitated, cleared his throat, then added, "Unless it rains." He paused again, then concluded, "In case of rain they will be joined up on the first clear Sunday." The following Sunday was clear and sunny, so promptly at ten o'clock all friends and neighbors gathered to see Uncle Christopher Columbus Hooks take unto himself a wife, a wife who, despite her rough and hardy personality, her lack of formal education, and her subsequent domination of him, was to hold his love and admiration for the rest of his life.

After their marriage Uncle Lum and Aunt Puss settled down on a little farm two miles from Spurger. They were still living there when I met the family. I was then seven years old; she was the mother of sixteen children, who ranged in ages from six months to twenty years. Her flock included two sets of twins. None of their children had left the nest at that time.

Marriage and the mothering of her brood had not interfered with Aunt Puss's work in the public interest. She was still the chief lookout or runner-down of Spurger's evildoers. It was not so much to punish them, but rather to teach them the way of truth, that she sought them out. Her close associates said that a soul was often saved while her biscuits burned and old Muley went unmilked.

One day when a rugged-looking stranger came to town to campaign for the office of sheriff, Aunt Puss informed him that she counted heads once every year and that Spurger now had two hundred citizens. "Two hundred and one," she corrected herself, "countin' my old hound dog Blister who does a pretty good job of rootin' out the loafers and any stranger who looks suspicious."

Aunt [5] *Puss*

In their capacity to multiply, Aunt Puss's kinfolks were like honeybees and rabbits. Besides having been just plain born, some of them must have been hatched and some grafted, because the landscape for twenty-five square miles was working alive with them. Occasionally, among them, you'd run across a queer-looking individual who, from all appearances, could have come from Mars. Take Cousin Pink Pettigo for instance. He was one of Aunt Puss's favorites, and he looked like he might have been one that sprang from a graft because he had the oddest thatch of beard that ever grew on a man's face. It looked more like brown pine needles than it did like hair, and he wore it in two neat braids that hung down over his shirt front.

The first time I saw Cousin Pink he was sitting in Aunt Puss's parlor. He smiled and said, "Howdy, little girl, you're mighty purty." I said, "Thank you, mister." Then I hurriedly left the room in search of Mama. I found her in the kitchen helping Aunt Puss prepare dinner. "Stop, Mama," I whispered, "stop churning the milk. I want to ask you something." I cupped my hand over her ear and said very softly so Aunt Puss wouldn't hear, "Do I have to be kin to the man in the parlor?" "I'm afraid you do, honey," she said. "He's one of our relations." I accepted this as a matter of fact, and from that day on I called him "Cousin Pink."

On Sunday mornings when the clan gathered in the little Methodist church to hear Brother Peabody expound the Gospel, they all wore their best behavior as well as their Sunday clothes. Even Cousin Pink wore his white shirt that day under his braided beard, and a celluloid collar around his neck. Whenever Brother Peabody said something that pleased him he would let go an encouraging "Amen!"

The grapevine communication system which served the territory where Aunt Puss's kinfolks lived, loved, labored, and died was more effectively operated than anything Mr. Alexander Bell ever strung upon poles.

Aunt [6] *Puss*

Sometimes hard feelings developed between the various factions, and then Aunt Puss was called in to mediate. But for the most part they all enjoyed close communion. And at the sudden unscheduled ringing of the church bell they could be seen streaming from their abodes like ants as they rushed toward a unified effort in behalf of whatever must be done to meet an unexpected emergency.

These people lived their lives with humility and gratitude, thanking their Heavenly Father every evening when they gathered in their various homes for family prayer. Few of them ever left their native habitat. Being content with what their present had to offer, they had no wish to peer into the future.

There was little need for them to rush from sunrise to nightfall because every day was likely to be a duplicate of the one just passed. They settled each day's problem before bedtime, then went to sleep with a clear conscience. Their years formed a circle which enfolded them with their joys and their sorrows, with the beginning and the fulfillment of their dreams—a circle broken only when their menfolk went out to fight for the protection and the preservation of their homeland. While life in the world moved on with ever-increasing tempo, time forgot them. But despite all their shortcomings and oddities, Aunt Puss, her friends, and her kinfolk made up a lovable, God-fearing aggregation of human beings, a people whose roots grew deep into the heart of the Southland. To this day I am glad I was one of them.

Spring Branch

Aunt [8] *Puss*

Uncle Christopher Columbus Hooks

UNCLE LUM was tall, thin and pale. His eyes were blue-gray. They looked at you with inviting kindliness that inspired trust.

After many children came to bless and disturb the quiet of his home, he could be seen at nightfall looking about for a place to sit down, relax, and read the volume of *Hamlet* his mother gave him after he married "the girl across the creek" and went to make a home for himself and family. Sometimes in the evenings after the children were asleep he read aloud to Aunt Puss, usually from Shakespeare. She liked to listen and she loved *Romeo and Juliet*. She said, "Lum reads real pleasin'. I'm glad he's got eggucation."

Uncle Lum was a melancholy individual—at least you'd think so from his looks. His face, in repose, was like that of a man who, like Lincoln, felt sympathy for all mankind. He usually wore an expression of calm resignation, appearing at times too weary to prolong the battle of life. He worked hard in the fields, and with the help of the older children he managed to give his family the limited comforts that poor people enjoyed in those days.

In keeping with advice given in the Good Book, when Uncle Lum felt like praying he went into a closet and talked with God. In this respect as well as in many other ways he was unlike Aunt Puss, who never made her prayers a private matter. Aunt Puss prayed all over the place; wherever and whenever the mood struck her, she let go an audible and all-absorbing appeal to the Almighty.

But the two did have something in common about things

spiritual: it concerned the souls of their offspring. Every Sunday the brood was scrubbed and polished to a shining finish, then crowded into the wagon and driven to Spurger to hear Brother Peabody preach in the good old-fashioned way that saved people from their sins.

Uncle Lum liked the finer things of life. Being aesthetic by nature, anything coarse or common repulsed him. When one of Aunt Puss's kin got in his hair and the pressure became too great, he'd go out to the smokehouse and take a few swigs of his homemade cherry cider. After that he loved everybody, even old Crum Toliver, the no-good cousin Aunt Puss had rather not have around because she thought him a bad example for her children.

Once Brother Peabody caught Crum making whiskey for sale on the sly. When Aunt Puss heard about it she said, "I'm awful 'shamed that he's one of my kinfo'ks."

When Crum came to spend the night at Aunt Puss's house and sat on her front gallery with Uncle Lum while she prepared supper, he spat amber tobacco juice through the space between his two front teeth and made a brown spot on the white sand in the yard. When he did this Uncle Lum always winced. Aunt Puss did keep spittoons around and it was something he'd rather not have seen, but he made no comment, for after all Crum was his wife's cousin.

But once late at night when Crum thought the family was sound asleep he went to the edge of the gallery and relieved nature by making a much bigger spot on the sand than he'd made with his tobacco juice. Uncle Lum was not asleep. The next day when he could no longer hold his peace he spoke to Aunt Puss about it.

After hearing of Crum's scandalous behavior, she stood for a moment rigid and silent, then she stomped her foot and her eyes flashed fire as she exploded, "If I wasn't a lady who is married to a gentleman I'd say the low-down sonova b-b-buzzard!"

Aunt [10] *Puss*

Aunt Puss Goes Visiting

MY FATHER, David Henry Wilson, was one of Aunt Puss's cousins by marriage. She used to say, "Henry'll make somethin' of hisself. He's the smartest one of the whole kaboodle."

After we moved to Plank it was hard for her to span the eighteen miles between her house and ours. But she was not one to let the problems of time or space defeat her. Before Uncle Lum bought the surrey with the black fringe on it he would take her in the wagon to Oscar Hook's place at Spurger. Oscar was her son, and he was the mail carrier who delivered mail in a rig very much like the proverbial one-horse shay. From Spurger she rode with Oscar to Hillister, which was fourteen miles in the right direction. From Hillister Aunt Puss walked about three miles, carrying her valise, until she reached Cousin Hank Willis's farm on Village Creek.

Cousin Hank was considered our well-to-do relation because he owned six mules and a buggy and his wife, Aunt Cynthia, used white linen tablecloths instead of oilcloth. Aunt Puss always spent the night at Cousin Hank's house and gathered some grapevine news to bring on to us. At daybreak the next morning Cousin Hank would harness old Jasper to the buggy and bring Aunt Puss on to Plank. When they stopped in front of our white picket gate she would crawl out, dragging her valise with her.

Now, Aunt Puss's valise was an interesting object. That it did not land in the Smithsonian Institution is that museum's misfortune. She had made the valise herself, with

Aunt [11] *Puss*

a little help from the blacksmith. It was fashioned from a pair of saddle-bags which Uncle Lum inherited from his family. Aunt Puss made the handle of bamboo strips, braiding them into a strong durable rope.

The valise was a two-in-one contraption. It looked exactly as it did years before when it straddled a horse's back. The handle was the only part which was not there when the horse wore it. One side was used for Aunt Puss's clothes, a calico Mother Hubbard, a yellow domestic chemise, a cotton flannel nightgown, and a pair of long, white knit drawers. The other side she lined with oilcloth for the "wets," and I don't mean baby diapers. Aunt Puss never carried any of her children with her when she went on a trip.

"I get enuff of the young'uns at home," she'd say. "When I go a-visitin' I don't want to wash hippens."

In the waterproof side of her valise Aunt Puss carried small rooted shrubs, which she wrapped in wet cotton-batting. She distributed these among her friends and relatives along the route of her travels. As soon as she stepped inside our front door she'd plunk down her valise and say, "Emmy, open it up and take out the wet plants for your ma." I loved doing this because I could peep into the other side and look at her clothes.

Sometimes she'd bring us several links of stuffed homemade sausage wrapped in her long white knits. When I saw such a bundle I'd secretly signal Mama. Then she'd give me a nod and wink, which meant, "Keep her out of the kitchen 'til after I've washed the sausage." The first time Aunt Puss brought us sausage she caught Mama washing the links in our dishpan and it hurt her feelings. After she went home Mama said, "Well, her drawers might have been boiled clean, but I couldn't take a chance on it."

Aunt [12] *Puss*

Aunt Puss at the Exercises

IN THOSE DAYS Spurger did not lack the benefit of drama, but sometimes it was of the raw variety. One night Aunt Puss and Uncle Lum sandwiched us all into the big wagon and we drove to town to attend the closing exercises of the community school.

There was much eloquence floating about the schoolroom that night, but what seemed to move on and on endlessly was "The Rime of the Ancient Mariner," which was read by a bespectacled youth who took his part quite seriously.

While I sat wedged in on a bench between Aunt Puss and Uncle Lum, I could feel her squirming with restlessness as the boy read his lines in a slow, monotonous voice while he repeatedly caught a long, loud breath with which to keep the ship moving. As he began the seventy-fifth stanza, "The loud wind never reached the ship,/ Yet now the ship moved on!" I felt a slight shudder pass through Aunt Puss's body, which occupied most of the left side of me. The shudder quivered itself to a standstill and I took a long, refreshing breath while the speaker continued, "Beneath the lightning and the Moon/ The dead men gave a groan." And just as the dead men gave that groan Aunt Puss squashed me again as she leaned over above my head and whispered to Uncle Lum in a clearly audible voice, "I wish the damn ship would sink!"

Aunt Puss Goes Dancing

ONCE Aunt Puss decided, October having come, she'd

Aunt [13] *Puss*

like to go to a dance at Spurger. "I want to go to a dance," she told Uncle Lum when he came in at noon from the cane mill. "Fall sort of makes me want to shake a foot." Uncle Lum looked at her warily. "Will you go with me, Lum?"

"I was afraid of that," he grinned. "Yes, I'll go with you if you're bound to go, but I'm getting too old to do a good job of shaking my foot."

I'll never forget how Aunt Puss looked when the children got through dressing her for the dance. She was wearing a purple albatross cloth dress and she had on high black shoes laced with strings she'd dyed the color of her dress. She'd made the dye from the juice of purple berries the children gathered in the woods. After her children finished their turnabout task of swinging their weight against her corset strings, she looked like an hourglass. They had tightened her to within an inch of her life and she was breathing with difficulty.

She wore a narrow band of black velvet ribbon around her throat. Attached to it was a gold locket. When Lucy, her sixth child, was fastening the ribbon at the back of her neck, she said, "Fix it good, honey, I wouldn't lose it for nothin'."

As she stood before the looking glass and gazed at herself she patted the locket and smiled. "The picture in it is the best one I ever saw of Mr. Abraham Lincoln." Remembering the life size portrait of Mr. Lincoln on the fire screen in Aunt Puss's parlor, I asked if he might be one of our kinfolks. "Lordy, no," she said. "He was a Yankee, but he was a good man and he done right when he freed the slaves. No human being was meant to be a slave."

After that she lifted a small spray of yellow and gold sweetgum leaves from a vase on the bureau and fastened it securely against her hair, which she was wearing in a

Aunt [14] *Puss*

knot shaped like one of her big biscuits on the top of her head. Now she was ready to dance.

From the way Uncle Lum gazed at her he must have thought she'd stepped right out of *Godey's Lady's Book,* a volume of which his mother had given him for his library when she gave him *Hamlet* and *Macbeth.* He wore his usual pale complexion that night and a tightly buttoned black vest. His red cravat was the only thing that kept him from looking like he was ready for burial.

Aunt Puss's Chickens

AUNT PUSS was proud of her chickens. With her big family to feed and the preacher on hand every Sunday, she considered them an economic necessity. She said, "Lum can raise the calves, the pigs, and the lambs, but I don't want 'im foolin' round the chicken house. He don't know nothin' about puttin' blue mass in their drinkin' water to keep 'em from having the sorehead and he don't know how to spray the chicken house with kerosene mix to keep the mites away."

One day Lucy, who was the pride of the family, came dashing into the house, saying, "Ma, that old Rhode Island Red has been off her nest an hour. She's not thinking a thing about the eggs getting cold." Aunt Puss dropped her knitting on the floor and started for the chicken yard in a hurry. "Them chickens is due to hatch out in five days," she grumbled. "Old Red is going to stay on 'em and hatch 'em out if I have to crawl in and set with her to hold her on the nest."

By the time we got to the chicken yard the hen was back on her nest, but until the little chicks were safely out

Aunt [15] *Puss*

of their shells I didn't go near the chicken house because I was afraid I might find Aunt Puss and old Red both on the nest and I knew this would outrage my sense of dignity.

Once on another day we heard a commotion out in the chicken yard and rushed out to see what was going on. Aunt Puss had just put her hand in a nest to pick up the fresh eggs and instead she had picked up a big chicken snake. Her noisy antics started the hens cackling and the roosters crowing. Like her husband and her children, Aunt Puss's chickens loved her, and when something unfortunate happened to her they resented it as much as if a hawk had swooped down and carried away a member of their chicken family. We got out there just in time to see Aunt Puss hurrying toward the woodshed with the long snake grasped tightly in her hand. She was holding him just below his head while the rest of him dragged behind her on the ground. She was angry and talking to the snake so fast we couldn't understand a word she was saying as we stood looking on with our mouths wide open and our eyes bulging.

When Aunt Puss reached the woodshed she grabbed an axe with her free hand, then laid the snake's head on a block of wood and chopped it off.

Aunt Puss and Religion

EARLY ONE MORNING Aunt Puss said to me, "The Miller baby just died. I'm goin' over to stroud it and lay it out, you want to go with me?" I looked at her with a question mark in my eye. Presently she said, "I reckon you ain't never seen nobody shrouded and laid out, have you?" Keeping my misgivings to myself, I went along. It was my first view of death and it frightened me.

Aunt Puss went about her task quietly and solemnly while I sat rigidly in a straight-backed chair and looked on. She bathed and dressed the baby, then laid it on a "cooling board" which was suspended between the backs of two chairs. We were alone in the room. Not one word was spoken between us until she closed the baby's eyes and placed a nickel on both of them. Then I began to sob, "I want to go home, I want to go home."

Aunt Puss said, "Well, I'm through now. Just let me speak to the family; then we'll slip out this side door and be on our way."

As we walked over the sandy road toward home Aunt Puss held my hand consolingly. After a while she said, "Child, maybe I shouldn't 'a brought you. You're scared." We went on a little farther in silence; then presently she said, "But, honey, I reckon it's just as well you learn early that life ain't always one grand frolic. Sometimes Ol' Mister Death walks right in where the fiddler's a-playin' and when he walks out he takes somebody with 'im."

When mealtime came around Aunt Puss wedged me in on a bench with one half of her brood while the other half sat on the bench opposite, facing us across the table. Uncle Lum, with his customary calm, would draw out the chair at the head of the table for Aunt Puss and then walk to the opposite end and take his seat. Presently Aunt Puss would give some authoritative gestures, which produced dead silence and the bowing of heads; after that she would begin a prayer, which she chanted in the manner of the late poet Vachel Lindsay. Her appeal was of such emotional force it made me tremble all over and fear that God might come right down through the roof to answer her in person.

One Sunday when the preacher came to eat Aunt Puss's fried chicken I gave him some illuminating information. He always said a lengthy grace. Aunt Puss showed him this courtesy even if her too abundant energy did force her to squirm in her seat before he said, "Amen."

The children sat at the big table with him. Aunt Puss didn't believe in pushing her flock aside when company was there. They never had to wait. Once I heard her say, "They're as good as the preacher. If he don't like to have 'em eat with 'im he'll just have to wait hisself."

But Aunt Puss made a mistake that Sunday when she put me just around the table corner from the preacher. I kept trying to be quiet, but he kept asking me questions. After while I decided to be sociable. I was short on vocabulary and subject matter, so I said the only thing I could think of at the moment.

"Brother Peabody," I hesitated briefly to get my wind and lay my fork beside my plate; then I looked straight at him and let him have it without benefit of comma, semi-colon, or period. "Brother Peabody, Aunt Puss says you pray too dog-gone long when we start to eat, and the reason you can't get your belly under the table is because you eat too many Rhode Island Red drumsticks."

Right here I ran out of breath and glanced at Aunt Puss. The awful look I saw in her eyes sent me hurrying from the table, saying to myself, "Jesus loves little children, Jesus loves little children. Please, Jesus, help me out of this sin."

After Brother Peabody left I waited quietly in the children's room to see what Jesus was going to do about it. Later I was sure he had answered my prayer because Aunt Puss looked at me sadly but did not say a word when we sat down at the supper table. That night, through a half-open door while I lay wide awake thinking about my sin, I heard Aunt Puss say to Uncle Lum, "I'd have switched the living daylights out of her, but her parents don't believe in corporal punishment." Finally I went to sleep wondering what kind of punishment I had escaped.

Aunt [18] *Puss*

The "little lamb" incident made a wound on my heart that did not heal for a long time.

To me there was something sacred about little lambs. I knew they belonged to Jesus because in the Bible he said, "Feed my lambs." Mama had read those words to me several times. She often read to me from the Bible, so at a very early age I was familiar with many quotations from the Good Book. But I learned after I was older that my interpretation of their meaning had sometimes been entirely literal.

One morning I went with the children to a place on Uncle Lum's farm I'd never seen before. They called it the "slaughter pen." I was horrified. Several little lambs had been killed and the men were cutting them into pieces, rolling the pieces in coarse salt, then packing them into containers and carrying the containers to the smokehouse. As the children watched the men work they jumped up and down gleefully saying, "Goody, goody, we'll have lamb stew tonight."

I managed to keep the quivery feeling inside me hidden until supper time. On the table that night were several bowls filled with lamb stew that lay in thick gravy. That was all except heaping plates of hot biscuits.

When Aunt Puss started to serve my plate I cried, "No, no, I don't want any."

"Child, what ails you? You ain't tasted it yet, you might like it." By this time I was wailing noisily, "I don't want any, I don't want any!" A little more severely Aunt Puss said, "Well, young lady, you'll have to eat it or go hungry—it's all we got."

"Then, please Aunt Puss, I'll go hungry," I sobbed. "I'd as soon eat Brother Peabody as one of Jesus' little lambs."

After that Aunt Puss never said another word to me, but she pointed toward the kitchen and nodded her head at Uncle Lum. "Please go in there," she said, "and fry this child some eggs while I wait on the rest of 'em."

Aunt Puss

Aunt Puss was as much at home in the pulpit as she was in the cowpen. She knew a lot about the Bible. Some of her neighbors said she could quote it from cover to cover with her eyes shut. She could not speak with eloquence, but there was a certain dignity about her when she preached a sermon or read aloud to her family from the Good Book. No one ever grew tired of hearing her read about Job and how the Lord tested him. Everybody loved the story of Jonah and the whale. Sometimes when she talked about fire and brimstone and the broad road that leads to hell the younger members of her flock could be seen edging up a bit closer to her, their eyes wide with excitement.

Aunt Puss was at her best whenever she took over Brother Peabody's pulpit while he was away from home or ailing. Once after his horse threw him and broke his leg she preached six Sundays in a row.

On the Sunday before Brother Peabody returned to do his own preaching, I was a visitor in Aunt Puss's home and went with the family to church to hear her expound the Gospel. Sitting with my mouth wide open in amazement, I watched and listened while she admonished her congregation to live in the love and fear of the Lord, and to close their ears and bind their tongues to the voice of gossip. "We must be forgiving and tolerant of them that stray from the narrow path that leads to salvation. My brothers and sisters," she pleaded, "be the last to cast a stone." She gave the story about the grain of mustard seed and declared that faith could move a mountain.

After we got home I challenged that statement, and when she looked at me as if she could not believe her ears, I said, "Well, I'd just like to see somebody try it. I'd like to see them move Dogwood Hill over on the other side of Spurger right up close to this house so we can see the flowers bloom every spring."

Aunt Puss turned away. As she took the hatpin out of her

hat she mumbled something about having Eula and Henry, my mother and father, teach their child more about the ways of the Lord.

In Brother Peabody's church the men and the boys sat on one side of the center aisle while the women and the girls sat on the opposite side. The first time I went to church with the Hooks family I wanted to sit with the boys, but Aunt Puss wouldn't let me. I didn't hear a word of Brother Peabody's opening prayer that day. All the while he was asking God to bless the people of Spurger and the nations of the world, I was peeping from beneath my leghorn hat at the boys across the aisle and resolving that by fair means or trickery I'd sit with them next Sunday.

After we reached home I announced my decision to Aunt Puss. She reacted emphatically, "Whoever heard tell of such a thing! A girl in petticoats sittin' on the men's side. Why, your uncle would be shamed to death." Aunt Puss convinced me somewhat that it would be an error but not enough. I would work out some plan by which I could enjoy fellowship with the opposite sex next Sunday. In fact, I might lay aside my petticoats if that was what bothered them.

The weather was only slightly cold the following Sunday when we started dressing to go to church, but I complained, "Aunt Puss, it's cold and my short coat is too thin. Can't I wear Lucy's long one?" I knew it would drag the ground because Lucy was much taller than I, but a long coat was exactly what I needed.

"It's too long," Aunt Puss declared. "You'll dirty the hem."

"No, Aunt Puss, I promise I won't; I'll hold it way off the ground." After some further discussion she gave in; then I got together my clothes, grabbed Lucy's coat out of the armor, and slipped out to the barn to dress. I didn't want anyone to see what I was wearing under Lucy's coat, because it certainly wasn't a petticoat. How fortunate, I thought, that Aunt Puss had a son just my size!

I realized that it was a somewhat daring thing which I was about to spring on Brother Peabody's congregation, but I never realized that I was to disgrace the Hooks family to the extent I did.

Arriving at the church, I walked erectly down the center aisle beside Aunt Puss. I managed to keep my secret until I slid safely inside the "off-limit for females section" and sat down by Uncle Lum, who had preceded us into the church. In surprised embarrassment he looked at me and said in an undertone, "Go right over there and sit with your aunt." My aunt was so occupied with her spiritual musings that she had not yet missed me. I didn't like the look in Uncle Lum's eyes as I whispered, "I can't." With his face now pink with humiliation, he whispered back, "Why can't you?"

I stood up, threw back Lucy's coat and faced him. "Because," I said in a clear, defiant voice, "I've got on britches and I can't sit over there with the petticoats."

By now the entire congregation had sensed something wrong in the men's section. Every eye was pinned on us as Uncle Lum wrapped Lucy's coat tightly about me, picked me up in his arms and made our inglorious exit.

"Why did you do it?" Aunt Puss asked me when she reached home. I could tell by her looks that she was hurt and humiliated. My voice trembled when I said contritely, "I'm sorry, I guess I just like boys better than I do girls."

"Well, don't ever do nothin' like that again. Your ma and pa will be mighty shamed when they hear 'bout it."

"I hope they won't hear about it. I promise never, never to do anything like that again." Perhaps they never did hear about it, because it was never mentioned again, at least, not in my presence. But Aunt Puss made sure that I wore a petticoat and dress thereafter when I accompanied her to church.

Aunt [22] *Puss*

Climax Pines

Aunt Puss had a silent way of controlling her offspring when one became restless during the sermon. She managed the youngest set of twins, who always sat next to her, by giving them a hard pinch. "I settle 'em down right now," she said, "by giving the pinch a good twist. It makes a blue spot on their bottom, but after they get the pinch with a twist they settle down and listen to what the preacher's sayin'."

Aunt [23] *Puss*

Aunt Puss Gets Lost

WHEN AUNT PUSS said she'd do a thing, nothing short of providential interference was likely to stop her. This is why all the kinfolks became alarmed when she didn't return home on a certain Friday afternoon as she promised when she started out to visit us after we had moved to Plank.

It was early one morning in May when she climbed into her surrey, picked up the reins, and touched Scamp lightly with her whip. As he trotted off she called back over her shoulder to her family, which had come out to see her off, "I'll be back next Friday about sundown if the Lord's willin'," and then she was off on one of her rare vacations. She arrived at our house late that afternoon after bypassing Cousin Hank's place.

After a brief visit with us, in keeping with her promise to her family Aunt Puss started home before sunup Friday morning. At twelve o'clock that night a horse and rider drew up in front of our gate. The rider, who knocked impatiently on our door, was Oscar Hooks. He'd come to see if Aunt Puss was still there. When told that she had started home before sunrise he said, "Sompin's mighty wrong. She ain't home yet and there ain't no sign of her or the surrey in sight of the road."

Mama made coffee for him; he drank a lot of it, then hurried away. Papa went out to the barn, saddled old Raven and followed Oscar. He wanted to help in the search for his cousin.

After Oscar rode into Spurger in a gallop, he went to the church and rang the bell. It was not yet daylight, but in a few minutes the citizens began rushing out into the darkness and were soon crowded about the church. After Cush told them something had happened to Aunt Puss, they started out in small groups to search the area between Spurger and Plank.

They found Aunt Puss just before dark the next day. After they took her home and made her comfortable, she told her family and friends the details of her misadventure.

Sitting with her feet in a tub of hot mustard water, she said, "I was drivin' 'long the road about ha'fway home when I heard to the right of me a cow lowin' in a mournful tone." She adjusted her feet to a more comfortable position and said meditatively, "I ain't never heard a cow low like that unless she was havin' a hard calf-birth."

Uncle Lum handed her another cup of coffee; she drank it, then went on with her story. "I drove off on a side road that led towards the sound of the lowin' but the road soon petered out into a pig trail and that ended in a thicket." Aunt Puss rested a minute. She still showed signs of fatigue from her ordeal.

"The cow was still lowin' ever now and then and I could tell I was gettin' closer to her. I got out and tied Scamp to a tree, got my rope and hatchet from under the surrey seat and started walkin' through the underbresh. I didn't have to walk long before I saw her." Aunt Puss's voice dropped to a sympathetic undertone, "Pore thing, there she stood jest lookin' at me, her eyes beggin' me to help. No tellin' how long she'd been there, stuck belly deep in a mayhaw bog, but she wasn't havin' a calf."

Tears rolled off Aunt Puss's face. "She was jest beggin' to be set free. I picked up some dead saplin's lyin' on the ground and throw'd 'em out on the bog; then I started workin' my way out to where she was standin'. I got nearly close enuff to wrap my rope 'round her horns—and then it happened." Aunt Puss shuddered slightly, "I slid right off into the bog myself, belly deep, right by her."

Presently Aunt Puss's eyes began to twinkle and the corners of her mouth turned up in a smile. "I know we was

Aunt [25] *Puss*

a sight, me and the cow, both stuck there cryin' for somebody to come and pull us out."

Uncle Lum patted her on the arm affectionately and said, "Honey, I know you were happy when you realized your folks had found you."

Oscar didn't give her time to answer. "I don't know how Ma felt," he chuckled, "but I know what she said when we got to the side of the bog. She looked up an' said, 'Get the cow out first—she's been here longer than me.'"

Henry Wilson Runs off with Eula Gilmore

ONE HOT, SUNNY DAY Aunt Puss spread her Lone Star quilt down on a shady corner of the gallery floor and said, "Now you young'uns lie down there on the pallet and take a nap." About six of us stretched ourselves out at various angles, and soon they were all asleep but me.

Just inside the room, near the open doorway, Aunt Puss sat carding cotton for a quilt she expected to put in the quilting frames the following day. There was a question I wanted to ask her and it was keeping me awake. Presently I got up off the pallet, went in, sat down on the floor near her chair and said, "Aunt Puss, will you tell me what that big noise was last night over at Mr. Kemp's farm?"

She looked up from her carding and listened to what I was saying. "It scared me so bad I put my head under the sheet and begged God to keep it away from our house."

Aunt Puss laid her cards down on the floor and looked at me. "Yes, honey, it was a shivaree, and I guess you never heard one of them things before in your life."

"No, Aunt Puss, I never did. What is a shivaree?"

Aunt [26] *Puss*

"Well, child," she said, "it's a heathernish kind of thing and there ain't no real sense to it."

I settled myself comfortably, looking straight at her because I could tell there was a story on its way. Then after a moment's silence, she said, "When a man and woman marries and goes home or wherever they aim to spend the night, their friends get set to give 'em a shivaree, and after dark comes on they all take pans and sticks and guns and anything they can make a noise with, and they march round and round the house where the bride and groom is. They keep the racket up until the groom brings his bride out to smile at 'em, say 'howdy' and take a drink of cider. Honey, that was what you heard last night over at the Kemp farm."

"Who got married?" I asked.

"Jack Kemp married the Cooper girl yestiddy, and brought her home to his pa's place."

"Does the bride and groom like the shivaree?" I asked. Aunt Puss chuckled, "I judge they don't like it, but they don't have no way of preventin' it."

"Did Mama and Papa have a shivaree when they got married?" I wanted to know. Aunt Puss laughed until she almost woke the children, "Lordy, Lordy, honey, there wasn't no time for a shivaree when they got married. But next day after the weddin' there was more noise let loose about it than a dozen shivarees could 'a made. Some sided with the Wilson family and some with the Gilmores."

"Did Mama and Papa make a mistake when they got married?" I asked.

"No," Aunt Puss replied, "it turned out to be the best thing they ever done. But the kinfolks didn't think so at the time." The children were still asleep on the pallet and Aunt Puss was in a talking mood, so I waited.

"Honey, ain't your ma never told you about how she run away with your pa when she was fourteen year old and him twenty-three?"

Aunt [27] *Puss*

"No, Aunt Puss, she never told me."

"Well, it's a long story," she said, "and it goes way back. Your pa had loved your ma ever since the days when she wore hippens and their two families lived on joinin' farms." A faraway look came into Aunt Puss' eyes as she continued. "Later, when she was a barefoot towhead and him a youth of twelve, he used to tote her across the fields so the grass-burrs wouldn't stick her feet. By the time your ma, who was little Eula Gilmore then, was twelve and your pa twenty, he'd made up his mind they'd be married when she was fourteen, and they sure was married."

Suddenly Aunt Puss stopped talking, got out of her chair, and went to the end of the gallery to get a drink of water from a bucket on the wash shelf. I sat quietly, hoping she'd come back and finish her story. Presently she came back, sat down and picked the story up where she'd left off.

"The marriage took place without either of the families blessin' it. You see, honey, the Gilmores had not been able to keep it secret that Indian blood flowed through their veins. They'd took the picture of old Swearingen, their Cherokee Chief ancestor, out of the family Bible, but not before somebody saw it and scattered the information about." Aunt Puss took a long breath and resumed. "Your Grandpa Wilson was a English gentleman and he was stuffed full of book learnin'. He swore out loud that he didn't want no redskin young'uns runnin' round his place. Your other grandpa, Jim Gilmore, was Irish and he roared that it made no difference how much learnin' old man David Henry Wilson's got, there sure didn't much of it spill over on his boy, 'the greenhorn that's married my girl.' But, honey, them two didn't give a half-chew of tobacco what nobody thought—red blood, blue blood, or no blood at all, them two had slipped off and got married."

Aunt Puss sat meditatively for a moment and then started talking again.

"One day in the summer of 1884," she said, "little Eula

Aunt [28] *Puss*

Gilmore took her book satchel and started to school as usual. Her books was in the satchel and so was sompin' else—it was her weddin' dress and shoes and hair ribbon, the same clothes she wore every Sunday to church." The children on the pallet were getting restless in their sleep. Flies were bothering them. Aunt Puss got up, fanned the flies off with her hand, then whispered, "Be quiet. If they wake up I won't be able to finish tellin' you about it! They'll be hollerin' about a drink of water and a cookie and raisin' a fuss generally." In a few minutes all was calm again and Aunt Puss picked up the thread of her story. "When mornin' recess come around," she said, "your future mother slipped away from the rest of the pupils and run across the creek where your future father was waiting for her under a sycamore tree. His horse was tied to the tree. He told her he'd look the other way while she changed her clothes. After that he buttoned her up the back and tied the ribbons on her hair, then put her on the horse in front of him and galloped away. Over on the river there was a log raft waiting for 'em—he had tied it up there that mornin'. They got on the raft and floated down the Neches River past Grapp's Bluff and Cherry Landing to the bend where your pa's cousin, Mary Williford, met 'em with her preacher, and right there on the river bank they was married. After the ceremony was over the preacher and his wife got on their horses and rode home and Mary Williford took the bride and groom back to her place near Kountze.

"Mary didn't want the old folks at home to be too worried, so she sent a runner to tell 'em what had happened, and that the bride and groom would be her company for a while.

"When your ma and pa went back to Spurger the families didn't welcome 'em very friendly. They hadn't got over bein' mad about the weddin', so in a few weeks your ma and pa packed their belongin's and left with some friends goin' west in a wagon train. And they kept travelin' in them wagons out on the prairie over a year, stoppin' and startin', couldn't

Pole barn with harrow

get satisfied no place they went. They covered many a prairie mile 'fore they set their faces toward home and it took 'em a long time to get back where they started from, and, honey, that's how come you was born in a covered wagon on the Texas plains."

Aunt [30] *Puss*

Uncle Faith

ONCE when I was visiting Aunt Puss she found Uncle Faith. She said she named him Faith because he had so much faith in God and man.

Uncle Faith was a Negro. He must have been ninety years old when Aunt Puss found him in a semiconscious condition in her front yard. It happened on New Year's Eve, when everything was covered with snow and cold winds whistled around the house corners in eerie gusts.

Late that night Aunt Puss's keen ear heard something more than the whistling wind. She crawled out of her warm bed, lit her lantern, and went out in search of a groan. Out in the yard she swung her light to the right, then to the left, and there he lay, flat on the ground near the gooseberry bush, an old man almost frozen to death.

Presently he stopped his mumblings, seeming to sense that somewhere above him was a voice that spoke comforting words. Aunt Puss hurried back into the house, shook Uncle Lum out of a sound sleep, and said, "Lum, get up quick an' help me bring in a poor old creature before he freezes to death. I found 'im in the snow."

They stretched the old fellow out on the floor in front of the kitchen hearth, then piled oak logs on the embers, which had been banked for the night. While Uncle Lum 'tended the fire and spread quilts over him, Aunt Puss made coffee and forced it down his throat. Before daylight came they discovered that he was totally blind.

During the weeks that followed the mysterious appearance of this stranger, his mind cleared sufficiently for him to enjoy the warm friendliness of the entire family, but his story was never told because he could not remember his name or anything related to his former life.

For several years Uncle Faith continued to be a happy member of the Hooks household. In due time he died, and his remains lay in a store-bought coffin right in the center of Aunt Puss's parlor while Brother Peabody read from the Holy Book.

When curious folks came to the graveside service, they saw the old man laid away in the Hooks paled-in plot. And some months later when they gathered for an all-day graveyard working, they discovered that the headstone at Uncle Faith's grave bore this inscription:

God Bless Our Friend
UNCLE FAITH

The Syrian Peddler-Woman

I LEARNED MANY THINGS from my remarkable aunt, among them lessons in tolerance, generosity, and kindness. One of these lessons concerned an old Syrian peddler-woman who made regular visits to Spurger. She knocked on Aunt Puss's door at least twice every year. Always she was weighed down with a heavy bundle which she carried on her back.

The woman was very dark-complexioned, and because she walked many miles over roads dusty in summer and muddy in winter, she was never tidy. But Aunt Puss invited her in and treated her as if she were a close friend. She always invited her to spend the night and eat supper with the family, and the woman never failed to accept the invitation.

After supper the peddler would spread out her merchandise on the floor in front of the fireplace, and the entire family would enjoy fingering her embroidered silk shawls and lace tablecloths. Aunt Puss would pick up some of her pins, needles, and ribbons; then when she started to pay for them the woman would wave her aside with, "You no pay, you good to me." But Aunt Puss always forced the money into her hand, saying, "Anybody who totes that bag all day earns her money."

Some of the citizens talked among themselves about Aunt Puss when they learned the peddler stayed with her overnight. "What will Puss do next?" they commented. "She takes in just anybody, sets 'em at her table and sleeps 'em in the room with her young'uns." When the gossip reached Aunt Puss it didn't ruffle her feathers in the least. "I know the Lord's will for me," she said. "As long as I got a roof over my head I'll share it with them that needs it."

The Dawsons

SPURGER got the first hint that it was to have some new citizens one morning when a dignified old man drove up in front of the general store, climbed out of a new buggy, and tied his chestnut horse to the hitching post.

Anthony Dawson was a six-foot, medium-heavy man with roving black eyes set back under heavy brows. He looked more like a Kentucky Colonel than a Yankee, but his accent betrayed him as one who had most likely fought against the Confederate forces, and this suspicion was confirmed later when a passerby noted a faded blue uniform sunning on a clothes line in his back yard.

After Mr. Dawson had fastened the bridle securely, he turned and said to a blonde, middle-aged woman he'd left sitting in the buggy, "Daughter, I'll be back presently." Then slowly he walked up the steps and into the store, where he exchanged greetings with Sim Carter, the owner.

"Anything I can do for you, stranger?" Sim asked.

"Yes, perhaps you can," the visitor replied. "I want some information. My name is Anthony Dawson and that is my daughter Julie out there in the buggy."

"I'm right proud to know you, Mr. Dawson," Sim smiled, "and glad to he'p you if I can." The man lost no time in stating the purpose of his visit. "I want to find a place where my daughter and I can secure room and board while I'm buying some land and building a home. And I'd like to find some carpenters."

"You aimin' to farm and maybe raise cattle?" Sim asked.

"No, I'm going to rest for a few years, just rest," Mr. Dawson replied.

"Have a drink," Sim said as he pointed to a keg on the counter that was conveniently tilted. "Thank you," the visitor nodded as he picked up a tin cup that was tied to the spigot in the keg, and drew himself some apple cider.

"Well, it looks like you've come to the right place, Mr. Dawson," Sim chuckled. "I can sure sell you some land and git you some carpenters that can build you a house, make the brick and dig you a good well to boot."

Mr. Dawson and his daughter were soon settled comfortably in the home of Miss Carrie Jordan, who boarded the school teacher and anyone else who needed to be boarded. At Julie's request Miss Carrie placed a small table near the south window in the dining room so that the two special guests could eat alone.

While under construction, the Dawson house attracted much attention. It was a big colonial that stood in a grove of elm trees just off the Woodville road a half mile north of Aunt Puss's home. No one in Spurger had ever heard of as many fixin's as were built into it. "Blamedest thing I ever seen," Crum Toliver told those who had not seen it for themselves.

Aunt [34] *Puss*

Long before Julie and her father moved into the new house, Aunt Puss called on them and made a bid for friendship, but Julie was haughty and disdainful. Aunt Puss told her friends, "I guess the poor thing is kinder lost down here amongst strangers who ain't her kind. She'll get over it after a while, and till she does we must be patient with her."

Soon after the Dawsons moved into their new home, a number of strange people appeared in Spurger. One of them was a blonde girl who spoke with a strange accent. Once when she went to the store to buy a writing tablet, Sim's curiosity got the better of him. "What brought you to these parts, Miss?" he asked.

"I am Mr. Dawson's housekeeper," she informed him, "but my home is in Sweden." A strange man had followed her into the store. She nodded toward him and said, 'That is Mr. Dawson's gardener." A number of other strangers from the Dawson household showed up at Sim's store from time to time and he liked every one of them. "They are sure more friendly than the folks they work for," he told his friends.

Many unspoken questions went unanswered as to why Anthony Dawson and his daughter had come to the little East Texas community to live among people whose ways were not their ways. But Spurger asked few questions. The citizens of this primitive town believed in the fatherhood of God and the brotherhood of man, so they waited patiently until Miss Julie was ready to become one of them. Years later a sudden, tragic incident brought about the thing for which they had waited.

Rebecca Sheffield Hooks

MRS. REBECCA SHEFFIELD HOOKS, better known as "Miss Becky," was Aunt Puss's mother-in-law. She was also my maternal great-grandmother. I can remember only four persons in her immediate family. They were Miss Becky herself, her two sons (Uncle Christopher Columbus and Uncle Noah), and Aunt Chlo, who was a much-loved member of the household despite the fact that her skin was as black as the ace of spades. Everyone said Miss Becky spoiled Uncle Noah because he was born when she was nearing the age of fifty. "A child to bless her old age," they declared.

Great-grandfather Hooks, who was Miss Becky's husband, died before I was born, but I can remember hearing old men with white beards say nice things about him.

Miss Becky was tall and gaunt, her face stern and solemn, and she seldom smiled. Her eyes were large, sky-blue and deeply set, her voice low and resonant. She usually wore a black alpaca dress trimmed at the collar and cuffs with narrow black lace. There was always a bunch of keys that dangled on a chain which was fastened to her belt. They were of no use whatsoever because there was not a closet in the house that had a lock on it. But the keys must have given her some feeling of security when she remembered that, as a child, before the Civil War, she had watched her mother use a key on this chain to open the lockers when they were full of silver and china.

Miss Becky spent much of her time sitting in the chimney corner smoking her pipe. She seldom mentioned the past, seeming to live in a world of solitude, a place within herself where she had at last found peace. She was not greatly interested in what those about her said or thought. Although advanced in years, she still had her own teeth, which were in perfect condition, but they were seldom seen because her lips were usually closed. Sometimes, when she removed her pipe from her mouth, I'd say, "Miss Becky, please smile so I can see your pretty teeth."

"Tut, tut, child," she'd mumble. "They might bite you." Then her face would soften into an embryonic smile which never quite found full expression.

It was a long time before she forgave Uncle Lum for marrying "the girl across the creek." But Aunt Puss's thoughtfulness and her forgiving nature finally won the confidence and regard of the dignified old lady.

Miss Becky's cook house was a long, low building. In it, at one end, was a big wood-burning cookstove and a small wooden safe that held the dishes. Against the side of the wall, under a small window that could be closed with a swing-shutter, was a table and on the table a cedar water bucket in which floated a gourd dipper. Against the opposite wall was a stationary ironing board, and above it a small shelf which held several smoothing irons. The homemade dining table was in the center of the room.

The floor of the cook house was pine and it was scrubbed to an unbelievable whiteness. It was covered with a thin layer of creek-bottom sand which absorbed all grease and food particles that fell on it. At regular intervals the sand was swept out and replaced with more that was clean and white.

On a covered path, halfway between the two buildings, there was a square, deep well that furnished water for the family. It was lined with red brick, which, near the curb, was covered with green moss. The cold water was drawn to the surface in a wooden bucket attached to a heavy rope.

Uncle Noah drew most of the water because Miss Becky thought Aunt Chlo was too old to do it. I don't think he liked it when Aunt Chlo called out too frequently, "Mastah Noah, water's out." Sometimes he'd bang down his book on the table and rush out with a scowl on his face, mumbling, "Dam-

Aunt [37] *Puss*

mit, one day I'll throw her in that well." I used to worry a lot about it, wondering just how Miss Becky and I would get her out if it ever happened, but it never did.

The milk house was the most interesting thing about the place. It was a small floorless room built directly over a clear, spring-fed stream which flowed just outside the back-yard gate. The water was usually about three inches deep, and it rippled gently over a pebbled bottom. The covered milk and butter pails were placed in the stream and weights laid on them so they could not overturn. Since the water that flowed constantly around these containers was cold, it kept their contents sweet and fresh. When a sudden rainstorm came up, there was much hurrying about to rescue the pails before they were washed away by the rising water.

Once when we were visiting Aunt Puss, Mama took me to spend the night with Miss Becky. Aunt Puss walked with us over the mile-long sandy road which lay between their two farms. Before we started, Mama looked at me and said, "Emmy, go put on your shoes. I want you to look nice when Miss Becky sees you for the first time." I'd heard a lot about Miss Becky and Uncle Noah, and now I liked the idea of spending the night with them.

When they saw us coming, both of them came out in the yard to greet us warmly. We went inside and laid the bundle containing our nightgowns on Miss Becky's bed; then all of us went out and sat down on the front gallery. In a little while I eased off my shoes and slipped away to see what I could find around the place. I went through all of the rooms, examining the furniture and punching the pillows to see if there was one I'd like to sleep on, until I selected the bed I wanted for mine. After that I started out to look for the kitchen. To my dismay there was none to be found. I never had seen a kitchen which was not attached to the rest of the house, and no one had ever told me about Miss Becky's cook house down in her back yard. It was growing late and I was worried. Presently I went back to the gallery. Aunt Puss was saying goodbye. I stood there and watched her walking slowly back up the road over which we had come, my heart growing heavy.

Suddenly, without a word, I grabbed my shoes off the floor, ran into the house and took my nightgown out of the bundle, rolled it up, tucked it under my arm, dashed past Mama on the gallery and started on the run to catch up with Aunt Puss. I could hear Mama calling after me, "Emmy, where are you going?" Without turning my head or slowing my speed, I answered her, "I don't want to stay there. I'm going back with Aunt Puss." Soon I caught hold of Aunt Puss's hand, then looked back and saw that Mama was not going to raise an objection, so I breathed easier. I felt Aunt Puss squeeze my hand as if she was glad I was with her.

"Emmy," she asked, "why didn't you want to stay with yo' ma?"

"I'll tell you why," I said, "but it's a secret. Promise you won't tell?"

"Yes," she answered, "I promise."

"Well, you see, Aunt Puss, while you were sitting on the gallery I looked all over that place." Then I tiptoed up to whisper in her ear, "They don't eat. They don't even have a kitchen." A broad grin spread over her face as I concluded, "I'm not staying at anybody's house where they don't eat."

Miss Becky died when I was nine. I remember the cold feeling of fear that gripped me as they lowerd her coffin in the ground and started shoveling dirt in upon it. Everyone sat motionless until the grave was filled; then Brother Peabody, who stood at the graveside with the Bible in his hand, said a prayer and led in singing "In the Sweet Bye and Bye."

By this time I had managed to crawl past Uncle Lum and run away. At the foot of the hill I climbed into the back seat of Aunt Puss's surrey with my teeth chattering from fright and bewilderment. After that it wasn't long until Aunt Puss,

Miss Becky—Rebecca Sheffield Hooks

Uncle Lum, and two of their boys came down the path and climbed in. Uncle Lum, in the front seat with the boys, picked up the reins and said with a quivery voice, "Giddap," to the horses. Aunt Puss, in the back seat with Lucy and me, picked up my hand and stared at me, saying, "Chile, are you sick? You look white as cotton." I didn't have the strength left to open my mouth.

"Don't feel too bad 'bout your grandma," Aunt Puss said consolingly. "All she had to do was to lay her pipe down, shut her eyes and let the Lord tote her 'cross the river." She paused to brush a tear off her face. "When she wakes up she'll be right there inside the Pearly Gates."

As we rode through the dusk over the tree-lined road, Aunt Puss kept talking reminiscently. "She never liked me much, thought I wasn't good enough for her son, but I didn't hold it against her, she was a good woman, she was. That's why I named one of my young'uns after her."

After Miss Becky died I never visited the old place and played under the "Sheffield Oak" again. Aunt Chlo, the faithful servant, died within the year, and it was not long before Uncle Noah joined them in the little graveyard.

Aunt [40] *Puss*

Uncle Noah

UNCLE NOAH, Miss Becky's pleasure-loving son, like Uncle Lum, his older brother, loved to read Shakespeare. He was tall and thin and he moved with great grace. His sharp, black eyes sometimes frightened me. They seemed to be reading my thoughts, which were not always complimentary to him. One day he looked at me searchingly and said, "Emmy, I don't want you to grow up at Plank and this God-forsaken place. It's too late for me to get out of here, but I want you to go somewhere and be somebody." His piercing eyes upset me. Hurriedly I answered, "Yes, Uncle Noah, yes, I'll surely go somewhere and be somebody."

Uncle Noah liked to ride fast horses, and while the family was still in a state of semi-poverty which had engulfed them following the Civil War, he managed somehow to keep a thoroughbred or two sheltered in the stable. He sat in the house when he was not riding the horses or reading books. Once when I went into the room where he was thumbing the pages of one of his books, he looked at me, held up the book, smiled and said, "Emmy, take a good look at this book; a great man wrote it. His name was Shakespeare."

When Aunt Chlo rang the dinner bell, Uncle Noah would walk slowly beside Miss Becky down the covered walk that lay between the main house and the cook house. At the head of the dining table he would draw out a chair for Miss Becky and stand there until she was comfortably seated. There were only two chairs at the long table, one at each end. At the sides of the table there were low wooden benches. Although the chairs were widely separated, Uncle Noah sat in the one opposite Miss Becky. After we were all seated we bowed our heads while Miss Becky asked God's blessing on the food we were about to eat, and on the family. Then Aunt

Chlo, tottering with overweight, would serve first Miss Becky, then Uncle Noah, while halfway between the head and foot of the table, on a bench, I waited my turn.

Aunt Chlo and Uncle Bill

AUNT CHLO and her husband, called Uncle Bill by the Hooks family, were the two slaves who decided to remain with the Hooks family after all the slaves were freed. I never saw Uncle Bill. He died before I was born.

Aunt Chlo was a familiar figure under the chinaberry tree in the back yard where she did the family wash. With a big stick she punched the clothes as they boiled in a large black iron pot. This was the same vessel she used to make soap from pork skins and other leftover fats in the kitchen. She kept the fire under the pot alive with dead limbs she gathered under trees in a nearby forest.

Aunt Chlo soaped the clothes, then laid them on the "battling block," which was a block of wood that had been sawed from a big oak tree. After she arranged a garment or two in a neat pile on the block, she beat the very life out of them with a stick that looked like a baseball bat.

Once Uncle Noah took me to see Uncle Bill's grave. It was not far from the one in which Grandpa Hooks lay. At the head of Grandpa Hooks' grave there was a slab of stone with his name, age, and the date of his death cut into it, but at Uncle Bill's grave there was a slab of wood painted white. On it in black letters was this inscription:

UNCLE BILL—FAITHFUL ON EARTH—

FREE IN HEAVEN

Aunt [42] *Puss*

Papa

ONCE when I was a small girl and Papa was past his mid-twenties, he said to Aunt Puss, "I been tryin' to make up my mind to jump the fence and find out what's out yonder. Spurger's shrinkin' and I want to do a little vagabonding." After that it wasn't long before he left his native home and went to work at Plank, the small sawmill town some eighteen miles away.

During his adult years, up to that time, Papa had been occupied with cutting pine timber off his land and floating it down the Neches River to Beaumont, where he sold it to sawmill operators. One of his customers, Mr. Joe Middlebrook, owned the mill at Plank. He liked Papa and soon they became good friends. Mr. Middlebrook urged Papa to move his family, which at that time consisted of Mama and me and my pet cow Jewel, to Plank and go to work for him.

Papa knew a lot about pine trees even then, but nothing about sawmills. Mr. Middlebrook said, "If you will do it, I personally will teach you the sawmill business from the ground up." And so it was that in the spring of 1888 we arrived at Plank. Mama then was eighteen years old, I was three, Jewel was eighteen months, and Papa, the only grown-up member of the family, was twenty-six.

Mr. Middlebrook kept his word literally about teaching Papa the sawmill business from the ground up. He gave him a wheelbarrow and put him to work as night watchman.

Mama and I used to take buttered biscuit and hot coffee to him every night about seven o'clock. We'd sit down on the ground and watch him in the glare of the burning slab-pit as he pushed his wheelbarrow full of sawdust and dumped it on a pile of slabs where so much had already been dumped it looked like a small mountain. When the wheelbarrow was empty he would walk over, sit down beside us, drink his coffee, and eat the biscuit we'd brought him.

One night he seemed unusually quiet. After a while he sighed and said, "Danged if I know whether I'm goin' to like this job or not. It's very monotonous. I'd rather be out in the woods treein' a bobcat."

Papa was gay and fun-loving. He had a sense of humor that was likely to break out suddenly at any time or place, but underneath his lively carefree exterior there was a strong decisive character. Much rugged living had etched deep lines on his honest face. His eyes blazed with anger when he saw evidence of cruelty and injustice. But he was tolerant of human weaknesses. Although Papa's intuitive judgment and keen business sense helped other men accumulate millions of dollars, he himself never had more than a few thousand dollars in the bank to his credit. Despite this fact, he was often referred to by his less well-off friends as a "rich man" because what he had was always ready for their use in a pinch. If a farmer needed enough to seed his ground, buy a pair of mules, or pay his doctor bill, Papa was standing by, ready to see him through. They usually called it a loan and a small rate of interest was charged; later the interest was or was not paid, depending on the debtor's ability to meet his obligation. In either case it was entirely all right with Papa.

Papa—David Henry Wilson

Aunt [44] *Puss*

Jewel

MY FIRST HEARTBREAK came soon after we moved to Plank. It concerned Jewel. When Aunt Puss gave her to Papa she said, "Henry, she's the finest Jersey calf ever born on our farm. I named her Jewel and some day she'll prove to you that she deserves the name." Soon Papa gave Jewel to me. Her soulful black eyes looked like pools of midnight. Men offered us a lot of money for her, but Papa always said, "No, she's a member of our family; not for sale." Because I wailed so loudly when we moved to Plank, Papa agreed to tie her to a rope behind the buggy and let her trail laboriously along in our wake.

Jewel was no ordinary cow. She should have been with a circus because she often made a spectacle of herself doing stunts, and she sometimes suffered physical injury as a result.

At Plank there was a long railroad trestle not far from our house. One day I was crawfishing in the creek that ran under the trestle. Papa stood nearby watching me. Jewel had followed us and while we were occupied with my fishing she decided to take a stroll on the trestle. She had covered some six feet of it before we heard the shrill whistle of an engine. It all happened in a second—the onrushing engine picked her up on its cowcatcher and threw her to the ground below at our feet. When we leaned over her she was not breathing; she was dead.

I knelt there sobbing, clinging to Papa's hand as he comforted me. "Come on, Honey, let's go home. I'll buy you another cow. She won't be an acrobat either, not if I can help it. Danged if I won't get you a cow that's got cow sense."

Mama

MAMA was a serene, gray-eyed woman with soft brown hair. I keep in my heart two pictures of her. The first is as she appeared to me when I was a child; then she wore a tightly buttoned basque and bustle. Her snug-fitting basque showed off her straight, slender figure, which narrowed to the proverbial hourglass waistline. Soft, pleated rushing edged the collar of her dress, making a frame for her heart-shaped face, which resembled a cameo.

Mama died when she was only thirty-five, but in my second picture of her she is not young. I see her body thickened by hard work and child-bearing and her face penciled with lines of care. But the eternal spirit of youth that is inseparable from courage, love, and faith in the good shone in her eyes, in the set of her lips, and the lift of her chin until the day she died. Here she remains in my mind the authentic picture of the pioneer mother.

Nature to Mama was the expression of God, His magnificence and simplicity. She saw His handiwork all about her. When I was thirteen, Papa planted his family in the deep solitude of a great pine forest where spiritual truths seemed to come to Mama spontaneously; the protective bark on the tall pines, the changing hues of the long-tailed chameleons, the warmth of sun after rain, all represented for her the goodness that is God. She talked with her children about these things and made lasting impressions on us all. She seldom appeared lonely, seeming to find ample companionship in the gray squirrels and the flash of a cardinal's wing. She asked for no music lovelier than the song of the wind in the trees. No opera or pageant could have stirred her as did the beauties of spring in the forest. I have seen her face light up with happiness at the sight of a hillside

Aunt [46] *Puss*

covered with wild honeysuckle blossoms. An acorn sprouting spoke to her of the Resurrection and the Kingdom of Heaven. A robin's nest tucked away in the branches of a sweet bay tree with blue eggs shining in a flickering pattern of sunlight made her eyes shine with joy. Like her father, she had a deep love of nature but her religious feelings were different from his.

Considering the background of Mama's religious training, received from her father, which was dogmatic and unyielding, picturing God as a relentless dispenser of quick and severe punishment, I have wondered how she ever acquired a more enlightened concept of the Almighty. She did take God and life with deep seriousness, finding little excuse for levity in daily living, but her unique spiritual sense somehow translated her father's stern God into a God of love and peace, just and merciful.

Because Mama loved music, she kept boarders for a while when we lived at the sawmill and saved enough money to buy an organ. She learned to play it by ear, hymns for the most part, but sometimes she would play "Over the Waves," "The Gypsy's Warning," and "My Bonnie Lies over the Ocean." Mama's children believed that she knew everything there was to know. She could always answer our questions about music, art, literature, and religion.

As I grew older I sometimes wondered about Mama's education, where and how she had acquired it after eloping and marrying Papa when she was fourteen. Perhaps she found it in her Bible and the many other books she read. She loved books and, while she had few of her own, her friends sent her many. Then when she had no books on hand she read the dictionary and the almanac. I remember the two monthly magazines she subscribed to every year; one was the *People's Home Journal,* the other *Good Literature.*

When I was fourteen the *Heiress of Hindee Hall* was being run as a serial in *Good Literature.* Every month I'd slip the magazine out, go down to Seiper Creek and, under the shade of a sycamore tree, I'd revel in the romance of the heiress and her poor unknown lover. After Mama found out about this, she hid the magazine where I couldn't find it. She said the story was entirely too grown-up for a fourteen-year-old girl.

Mama used to order patterns and dress goods from the Baird Company in Shreveport, Louisiana. She kept herself and her children neatly dressed, even though our clothes were seen only by the wild animals. I think she and Mr. Baird became very good friends by letter because when she sent him an order she'd add a personal note saying, "Mr. Baird, will you please send me a good book to read and include bill for same?" Then along with the material and the bills Mr. Baird would send a note, "Dear Friend and Customer: I hope you like the book I'm sending; I haven't read it yet but it's said to be very good."

Mama always liked Mr. Baird's books, but once I think he must have left the selection to one of his young employees. I can't remember the title of the book, but it must have been a naughty piece of literature because Mama closed it suddenly after she'd read a few pages, then rather wistfully she said to herself, "I wonder what's happened to Mr. Baird?"

Mama—Eula Gilmore Wilson

Aunt [48] *Puss*

Ellie

ROSELLA GILMORE was my maternal grandmother. She was better known to her family as "Ellie."

Ellie was a small, gray-haired woman with sharp blue eyes that could look right through you when you'd done something wrong. She was stoop-shouldered and thin and her face was full of wrinkles, but she could outwork any other member of the family. I remember her best as she labored in the kitchen, lifting heavy lids off iron pots so she could dish up the turnip greens. And as she lifted a cup to her mouth, she held it with both her palsied hands so the coffee wouldn't spill over.

Ellie had an ingrown fear of accidentally putting a garden worm in the pot with her vegetables. She wouldn't let the children come near when she was "looking the greens" for fear they'd divert her attention and cause her to miss a bug or worm.

She had a great dislike for milk in any form. The odor of it made her deathly sick. She kept her personal dishes on a shelf to themselves and washed them separately from those of the family.

Ellie's summerhouse out in the garden was the place I loved. It was my make-believe home where I kept my dolls. It was octagon-shaped, enclosed with latticework and covered with honeysuckle vines. It was a place in which I could dream big dreams of a far-off world which was already beckoning me.

The neighbors said Ellie had a "green thumb" because everything she planted grew into something beautiful. When I was six years old Ellie set out a dozen young apple trees, but they never grew one inch because on the following day, which was February twenty-second, she told me about

George Washington and his hatchet. Immediately after she finished the story I went out and chopped down every one of them. Then I went back into the house and abruptly told her about it.

"Ellie, I am truthful just like George Washington. I cut down every one of the apple trees."

She looked through me for a moment; then she started crying. It hurt me through and through because I'd never seen her cry but once before; that was when her eighteen-year-old son Manny died.

Ellie used to make sassafras tea and give it to me in the spring to "purify my blood." In winter she made me wear around my neck a ball of asafedita tied to a string. "It's good to keep diseases away," she said. I seldom rebelled when she doctored me, not even when she poured sulphur and molasses down my throat. But once when I was ten years old she approached me with a tablespoon in one hand and a bottle of Lydia E. Pinkham's Vegetable Compound in the other. Then I put up a fight.

"I will not take it! I will not!" I shouted.

She had never before seen me in this mood. She sat down in a chair, then said, "It's not a bad dose. Why won't you take it?"

"Because I'm too young," I answered. I saw that she did not understand, so I told her bluntly, "Mrs. Simpson says there's a baby in every bottle and I don't want to have a baby right now."

Ellie went back to the kitchen with the spoon and the bottle in her hand. As she placed Lydia E. on the medicine shelf I overheard her say, "What a child! What a child!"

Ellie used snuff; sometimes she sniffed it up her nose and sometimes she used a snuff-brush. I used to go to the woods with her to get blackgum twigs for her brushes. She'd peel the bark off the little stick, chew the end of it, dip it in the snuff bottle, and then put it as far back in the side of her mouth as she could. It seemed to give her so much satisfaction that I decided to take up dipping. I'd tried the sniffing and didn't like it because it made me sneeze.

One day I took Ellie's chewed snuff stick and her bottle of snuff and went back of the house, hid myself between the rows of full-grown cotton, and settled down for a dip, following Ellie's routine. The snuff had a sweetish taste that I liked. Yes, I thought, dipping is very nice. That was the last thought I had for quite a while. When I came to my senses I was deathly sick, lying on a bed in the house and my two aunts and Ellie with cold wet cloths were trying to bring me back to life.

Ellie was a true pioneer mother and grandmother, unselfish, kind, and wise. I never drive by a farmhouse at night and catch the odor of honeysuckle growing on a fence without remembering Ellie's summerhouse where my dreams began.

Pappy

MY MATERNAL GRANDFATHER, James William Gilmore, called "Pappy" by his children and grandchildren, loved Christmas time.

He was a man of peace, but he never did stop fighting the Civil War. When his friends said, "Mr. Jim, you hadn't oughta hold a grudge so hard," he'd stroke his clipped beard, look at them with a twinkle in his blue Irish eyes, and say, "I've got no grudge. I buried the hatchet a long time ago." Then, with a chuckle, he'd add, "But I left enough of the handle stickin' out for me to grab if a Yankee ever comes down here and gets sassy." (And incidentally, he had lost a finger at the Battle of Mansfield.)

Pappy was the grandson of a Cherokee Indian Chief who ruled his tribe near Colquitt, Georgia. It was at Colquitt that Chief Red Leaf (Swearingen) met and married the white woman who grew on our family tree. Pappy inherited many Indian traits of character from the chief. Among them was his ability to remember any act of kindness shown him or his family, and his eagerness to repay in kind. And just as clearly remembered was any act of unkindness or injustice. His great love of nature, especially the great forest, may have been handed down to him by his Indian forebears. He seems to have passed it on to my mother.

Pappy always led the singing in his church. And in the amen corner where he sat, his musical hallelujahs often punctuated the preacher's remarks.

I'm afraid the family did not fully appreciate his voice until one day when we heard him read a letter the mail-carrier brought him. The letter was from the pastor of a little church some forty miles from Spurger. The letter read:

Dear Brother Gilmore:
My little church at Rockland is not able to buy an organ. I am told that your voice cannot be distinguished from organ music .... It would be our pleasure if you would take the place of an organ at our Sunday morning services. There would always be lodging and feed Saturday night for your horse and yourself.

      Respectfully,
      Joshua Reed, Pastor

For many years Mama kept this letter in her Bible.

After Papa moved his family to Plank, Mama often took us back to spend Christmas with our grandparents. The day before Christmas Eve, Pappy would take us to the woods to look for a Christmas tree. We would walk beside a rippling stream because he said the best trees grew near the water. After a while he'd take the axe off his shoulder, lay it on the

Aunt [52] *Puss*

ground and start singing in a low musical voice that gradually rose in volume until it sounded like a great organ. To this day I say to myself when I hear a great pipe organ play, "That is Pappy's voice."

Once I said to Pappy after I heard him sing by the creek, "Why do you always sing when we stop by the creek?"

"Because," he replied, "the creek taught me to sing."

Mama, Aunt Jennie, and Dollie always decorated the tree with long strings of white popcorn and red cranberries. There was always a red candle tied at the tip-top, which was not lighted until Christmas morning after we went in to receive our gifts off the tree.

The presents never varied in quantity or quality. There was a stocking for each child filled with nuts, rock candies, an apple, an orange, and for the girls a baby doll wearing a long white dress. The doll's head was always peeping out above the top of the stocking, and beside it there was a stick of peppermint candy. Instead of a doll, the boys found a "bean shooter" and candy sticking out of their stockings. There was also tied to the tree for each child a white china mug with flowers or birds painted on it.

Before the presents were removed from the tree, Aunt Dollie would play the organ and we would all stand and sing Christmas songs. After that, Pappy and all of us would sit down. Then the children became very quiet while he wiped his eyeglasses with extreme care before putting them on. When they were adjusted exactly to his liking, he took his Bible from the table at his elbow, opened it and started reading aloud the story of the Babe of Bethlehem.

Pappy was rigid in his rules concerning the company his daughters kept. When they were going out to attend a spelling bee, a candy-pull, or a cobweb party he must know who their escorts were to be. And he always appeared in the parlor doorway before they left to say, "Be back home by nine o'clock."

Aunt [53] *Puss*

In those days of no telephones, dates were made by means of notes delivered by little boys. Aunt Dollie was the baby of the family. At sixteen she was beautiful, and she attracted much admiration from the young beaux about town. One Saturday morning she went to the general store and was introduced to a handsome newcomer. The stranger was the first dentist to establish practice in Spurger, and he was there for the purpose of opening his office.

Late that afternoon, his note was delivered to Aunt Dollie's house. As was his custom, Pappy opened and read the note before he passed it on to Aunt Dollie. He was apparently greatly impressed. "I never before," he said, "read anything written in a more manly way." The note read:

Miss Dollie Gilmore:

May I have the pleasure tomorrow evening of supporting your corporal system along the space intervening between your parently domicile and the First Methodist Church?

Respectfully,
Homer Beckett

Aunt Dollie did not marry the dentist, but she kept his note among her souvenirs as long as she lived.

I learned many things from Pappy and his way of life. He didn't spill over with friendliness nor wear his heart on his sleeve. But he was all wool and a yard wide. He loved Christmas time more than anyone I've ever known to this day.

Aunt [54] *Puss*

Pappy —James Williams Gilmore

Aunt [55] *Puss*

Aunt Sue and Uncle Bob

AUNT PUSS used to say, "I reckon Sue and Bob is the porest kinfolks I got."

Uncle Bob was Papa's younger brother, but you'd never have known it from his appearance, his manner, or his reaction to life's problems. He was six feet four and stoop-shouldered. His arms were unbelievably long. Standing on the ground, he used to reach up and straighten the shingles on the eaves of his lean-to roof whereas any other man would have needed a ladder. In repose Uncle Bob's face radiated good humor. His soft brown eyes had a twinkle that came and went as if some secret thought furnished him amusement.

His besetting sin was laziness. He had inherited a creek-bottom farm from his father but he never could find time or inclination to work it. The sleek team of mules Aunt Puss gave him grew thinner and thinner because he forgot to feed them. Then, when their ribs began to show through, he declared, "I just ain't got the heart to plow Maude and Mack today 'cause they're too pore."

Aunt Sue managed to keep food in the house by raising chickens and selling eggs. But it was a mile to the market at Spurger and Uncle Bob said it was too far for him to walk on his bunion, so once a week Aunt Sue walked to town and brought back the groceries and Uncle Bob's Virginia twist.

Aunt Sue was short and fat. Her right eye tooth was missing, and when she got mad at Uncle Bob and talked at him very fast, a whistling noise punctuated her words while her black eyes rolled round and round. At other times when she was "too put out" for words, she'd just look at him steadily with her eyes wide open. When he could bear her piercing stare no longer, he'd say, "For God's sake, Sue, shut your eyes. They look like muscadines in a bowl o' clabber."

One day when Aunt Puss paid them a surprise visit, she found Uncle Bob asleep in his rocker on the gallery and Aunt Sue in the hot sun hoeing potatoes. In disgust she went to the potato patch, took the hoe from Aunt Sue's hands and said, "Sue, if you'd fire a pine knot and set it under Bob and his rocker maybe he'd get up and start a crop and buy a sausage grinder and some cotton cards you've been needing so long." But Aunt Sue never did light the pine knot.

Once Papa persuaded Uncle Bob to rent out his farm and move to Plank to work in Mr. Middlebrook's sawmill, where he had reached the important position of foreman.

A little house was made ready for them not far from where we lived. When Aunt Sue walked into it she said, "Praise the Lord, I feel like I've died and come to heav'n." She loved the white lawn curtains Mama had put up at the windows, and the coffee grinder that was fastened to the wall back of the cookstove. She beamed at Papa, "A rose bush by the front gate and glass winderpanes where I can see the rain fallin' down." Her former home had wooden shutters at the windws. It was hard to tell just how all this affected Uncle Bob as he sat down in his rocker, stretched his long legs and sighed. That sigh could have meant any one of a number of things.

When Aunt Puss heard what Papa had done she wrote him a letter. "You laying yourself open to a lot of disappointment if you aiming to reform Bob. Godamighty ain't been able to do it yet."

Soon after they were settled in their new home, Uncle Bob went to work at the mill. For a while Papa had high hopes that he would throw off his inertia. At first he put Uncle Bob, who had never seen a sawmill before, to hauling discarded bark and strips of refused lumber to a place where it was drawn up by heavy chains, dropped into the slab-pit and burned. But all too often Uncle Bob's wheelbarrow would be found empty on the dollyway and Uncle Bob would be found asleep under a nearby tree. On being rebuked he would say, "Seems I just got tired all of a sudden."

Papa taught Uncle Bob how to scale logs on the skidway, but he complained that he had to bend over so far it hurt his back. He was changed from the skidway to the millpond to float logs and guide them, one at a time, to the lift, which drew them up and placed them on a carriage which took them to the circular saw that cut them into lumber. In a few days Uncle Bob said to Papa, "I just cain't do this job 'cause floatin' on the water makes me dizzy."

Papa's patience was wearing threadbare. He was ready to concede that Aunt Puss knew what she was talking about, that not even Godamighty could reform Uncle Bob. But Aunt Sue was so happy in her new life Papa hated to send them back to the farm. She had joined the quilting circle and her days were filled with happy anticipation as she waited for the arrival of her first baby.

Uncle Bob was like a new man after little Sue came. He actually worked uncomplainingly and rarely lapsed into his former idle habits. No one knows what the outcome might have been had not tragedy struck his heart and home.

Little Sue, six months old, blonde and lovable, became ill of diptheria. Three days later I saw Papa drive up to Uncle Bob's gate in our shiny new buggy drawn by a black horse. He got out and went into the house. Then Aunt Sue, wearing a black dress and a long black veil on her black sailor hat, came out leaning on the arm of the Methodist preacher. He helped her into the buggy, where she sat motionless and mute, staring straight up the road.

Next Papa came out walking beside Uncle Bob. In his arms Uncle Bob was carrying a little coffin painted white. They passed single file through the gateway; then Uncle

Aunt [58] *Puss*

Bob silently walked to the side of the buggy where Aunt Sue was sitting and placed the coffin on her lap. After that he turned and bowed his head in a wordless good-bye to Papa and the preacher. With his face drawn by grief, he walked to the other side of the conveyance, climbed in, picked up the reins from their fastening on the dashboard and slowly drove away.

Aunt Sue and Uncle Bob started on their eighteen-mile drive with their precious baby just as the sun rose above the treetops. It would be casting shadows before they reached Aunt Puss's house, which was a mile from the little hillside graveyard.

Astride a limb in a crepe myrtle tree, I watched the buggy until it disappeared around a bend in the road. My heart was overflowing with sorrowful emotion.

Aunt Sue and Uncle Bob never returned to Plank. They said they wanted to stay on the farm where they could put flowers on little Sue's grave every Sunday. The next time I saw them I was a grown-up woman with a son of my own.

Miss Kate Sawyer

MISS KATE SAWYER came to Plank after Papa's sawmill career was well on its way to success. Judged by the social standards of today, Miss Kate would be a prosaic old fogey. But at Plank in the mid-nineties she was quite a girl. "Fast," the women declared as they tried to steer clear of her contaminating influence.

Miss Kate wore her blonde hair piled high on top of her head with gay combs tucked in at saucy angles to keep it in place. Her skirts were so short you could all but see her ankles when she walked fast and the wind fanned her petticoat ruffles. She beamed a broad smile at every man she passed and said, "Good morning," even if she'd never seen him before.

One day when Aunt Puss was visiting us, our neighbor, Mrs. Grissom, said to Mama, "That bold Kate woman is a hussy." Mama glanced at Aunt Puss uneasily as Mrs. Grissom continued, "Did you see her come in and sit down in the church house last Sunday night and cross her legs just like a man?" Aunt Puss bristled, "Maybe she just wanted to get herself settled comfortably so she could pay attention to the preaching." It was easy to see that Aunt Puss was going to defend Miss Kate.

"Well, I do say!" Mrs. Grissom glared at Aunt Puss. "You takin' up for her?" Aunt Puss was thoughtful and silent for a moment, then quietly she said, "I was just thinking maybe we'd better let Godalmighty take care of the judgin' without too much help from us mortals who don't rightly know what's in the woman's heart." Mrs. Grissom swelled up and shut up, but from the edge of her high, tightly buttoned collar to the hairline on her forehead she was beet colored.

That night I caught Papa's attention long enough to say, "Papa, what's a hussy?" He gave Mama a look out of the corner of his eye and replied, above a chuckle, "Danged if I know. Ask your Ma." Over in the corner Aunt Puss was shaking with suppressed laughter. The following Sunday she invited Miss Kate to attend church with her, and Miss Kate accepted.

It was quite a while before Miss Kate interrupted the calm routine at our house, and then it was not her fault. It was the result of an invitation Papa gave her to "come over."

Papa and Mr. Furby had bought a phonograph. It must have been the great, great grandpappy of radio. It was the first "talking machine" seen and heard in our part of the country, and it caused something of an uproar. The two men formed a partnership through which they hoped to make some money. They hired a man to take the machine to towns up and down the railroad and collect money from people who listened to it perform. They had about a dozen cylindrical records of songs popular at that time, and there was an attachment with which they could make other recordings. The machine, or phonograph, was enclosed in a shiny black box that was somewhat smaller than an apple crate. From each side of the box came four rubber tubes about forty inches long. Attached to these tubes were black gutta-percha nozzles which you stuck in your ears if you wanted to listen to the thing perform.

Now, Miss Kate had a voice; the women doubted it but the men didn't. They knew she could sing like a mockingbird because they had heard her do it. I'm sure Papa had the commercial side in mind when he invited Miss Kate to our house to record a song on his talking machine, but he certainly made a mistake when he forgot to tell Mama she was coming, and a much bigger mistake when he let her start to warble before he invited Mama in to listen. Mama didn't like it a bit when she heard Miss Kate in our parlor singing "Watermelon Smilin' on de Vine."

I was standing near Mama at the cooktable in the kitchen where she was peeling Irish potatoes to cook for supper. When that voice drifted in across our cookstove, I saw a shadow, dark as night, spread across Mama's face. I knew right then that Papa had made the biggest blunder of his life.

My parents seldom argued about anything in my presence, but I always knew when they started ignoring each other that something corroding was in the wind, and usually before the air cleared Mama would take me to visit Aunt Puss.

The next day after Miss Kate recorded the song for Papa, Mama and I went for one of those visits, and we stayed longer than usual.

Aunt [61] *Puss*

Morogan's Terrible Men

THERE are many memories of our life at Plank that come back to bring a laugh or a tear.

One is of the day our home burned to the ground and school was dismissed so the pupils could watch the fire. Wildly, I ran with the other children toward a column of black smoke that was rising skyward, only to be halted by paralyzing fear when I was close enough to see that it was my own house burning down. What stopped me in my tracks was the sight of four men carrying Mama out of the burning building on a stretcher made of bed quilts, while our neighbor, Mrs. Furby, walked beside them holding in her arms my infant brother, who had been born only the night before.

I remember, too, that it was in the schoolhouse at Plank that I appeared for the first time as a public speaker. I was eight years old then. I had completed *McGuffy's Fifth Reader* and could spell correctly every word in the *Blue Back Speller*.

Papa boasted, "Only a smart young'un could do that." And I believed him until the school season ended in the spring of 1893 and I was selected to recite Constance Fenimore Woolson's "Kentucky Belle" at the closing exercises.

On the night of the recital, after I was dressed in my pretty blue lawn costume, Papa looked me over proudly.

"Honey, your dress is a little short," he complained.

"Not as short as Sallie Tucker's," I assured him.

"Danged if I ain't proud of you and the way you look tonight." My morale rose to a high pitch as he beamed at me, "Honey, don't you be scared. You're smart, you go right out on that stage and show the folks what you got." Poor Papa, little did he realize how completely I'd show them what I had.

Aunt [62] *Puss*

At the appointed hour the doors of the schoolhouse were thrown open and soon every bench in the room was occupied to capacity. My family managed to get on the front row so they'd have a good view of me. Joe Bentley, part owner of the mill but not yet a millionaire, sat there with them.

First on the program was a salute to Old Glory by the entire cast; next came the singing of the "Star Spangled Banner." After that the professor gave an inspirational talk on the importance of education for young Americans. Then two acts followed in smooth succession. First came the simultaneous reading and acting of "Curfew Shall Not Ring Tonight." In this act Sally Tucker clung to the bell-clapper as the bell, which was suspended from the ceiling, swayed back and forth about six feet above the stage floor. As I watched from behind the stage, through a knot-hole, I could see that Papa was not liking Sally's short skirt as her long, skinny legs dangled clumsily.

In the second sketch there appeared a boy dressed as Daniel Boone. He was seen killing a wildcat with his bare hands. After disposing of the cat he was about ready to send an obstreperous Indian to his Happy Hunting Ground when someone accidentally lowered the curtain and hid from view the gruesome deed.

Now it was my cue. With extreme confidence and rare elegance I walked to the center of the stage, and, under the light of a swinging kerosene lamp, began reciting "Kentucky Belle." Slowly at first, but with ever-increasing tempo, I related the story of a magnificent horse and the part she played in the Civil War. By the time Morgan and his men came into the picture I sounded like a spring freshet dashing down the mountainside.

Morogan, Morogan the raider and Morogan's terrible men
With Bowie knives and pistols are galloping up the glen!

Aunt [63] *Puss*

I became brilliantly inspired as the cavalrymen raced madly across Georgia. By this time my arms were flying around in circles while my feet did taps on the floor, imitating the the sound of galloping hoofs. Even in my excitement I coordinated my faculties sufficiently to think, "Papa will be proud of me now." I began to cool off and slow down a bit when I reached some less agitating lines.

> The lad rode down the valley
> And I stood still at the door,
> The baby laughed and prattled
> Playing with spools on the floor.

But the damage had already been done. My strenuous gesturing had sprung a drawstring.

I felt something loosen at my waistline and drop to the floor. My tongue froze in my mouth, my feet stuck to the rough planks beneath them. I looked at my family—my four-year-old brother had risen from his seat. He was pointing his finger straight at me as he shouted, "Look! Papa, look! Emmy's lost her drawers!"

Suddenly I felt as if a bucket of scalding water had been dashed on me, unfreezing my feet and legs. Turning, I started to run, but my drawers hobbled my ankles. I took only two steps before they brought me down, sprawling on my stomach. I lay there for an instant in the midst of profound silence. Not an audible chuckle could be heard above the deathlike quiet. Then my brother began to cry. But people can be kind. Some dear soul let down the curtain and hid from sight all that was left of Mr. Wilson's "smart young'un."

The next day when Joe Bentley came to our house I could see that he was biting his tongue to hold back a smile as he said to me, "Damned if I ever saw a better show in my life, and you sure know how to recite poetry."

"Thank you," I murmured guiltily when he handed me

a five-dollar bill and said, "I want you to buy yourself a nice present with this."

Even after I was a grown-up woman I never let Joe know that I overheard him when he whispered to Papa, "Damned if I didn't bust two buttons off my vest last night trying to hold in a laugh."

Macbeth in Beaumont

WHEN I was ten years old Papa took me to Beaumont to see *Macbeth*. One day I heard him say to Mama, "Eula, I don't want Emmy to grow up green like me. I'm goin' to give her some advantages an' I'm goin' to start doin' it right now because she's already ten years old."

He took a small yellow circular from his pocket and handed it to Mama. She didn't look at it at first. She kept on looking at him and listening.

"The conductor throw'd a bunch of 'em off the train this morning," Papa said. "It's sompin' about a theatre show called *Macbeth*." Then, for the first time Mama looked down at the circular in her hand while Papa kept on talking.

"It says, order your tickets today by mail. I'm goin' down right now and order 'em." As he went over to take his hat off the wall peg, Mama said, "What'll she wear?"

"What she wears don't matter," he answered over his shoulder. "What matters is that she gets some advantages before she gets too old for 'em to do her any good." Then as the distance widened between them he said, "Sorry you can't go with us, Eula." Mama had not been invited because she was "expecting" and in those days that was synonymous with solitary confinement. Ladies simply didn't go outside their own yards when they were in "the family way."

Aunt [65] *Puss*

Mama made me a new dress and bought me a new hat. Two weeks later I was on the train with Papa. We were on our way. I was wearing my new sprigged challis and my leghorn hat. Papa wore a white celluloid collar and a black bow tie. As the train rumbled along I looked at him and said, "Papa, you're looking good today. You look just like Mr. Abraham Lincoln."

"When did you see Mr. Lincoln last?" Papa laughed.

"Oh, I never did really see him. I just saw his picture in Aunt Puss's locket and on her fire screen under the mantel. And, do you know, Papa, everywhere I'd go in the room his beautiful eyes followed me. I think he wanted to talk to me but he didn't know how."

"What about his beautiful nose?" Papa laughed again.

I didn't have time to answer that question because the train was moving into Beaumont. Already street lights were shining through the coach windows and I was quivery with excitement. It was about nine o'clock when we reached the little boarding house where we were to stay, the same one where Papa stayed overnight when he used to float his logs down the river to sell in Beaumont.

The next morning we were up early, ready to start out to see things. As we walked toward the gate, Papa pointed to a little house near the back fence and said, "Honey, before we leave, you'd better go to the outhouse." He knew I'd never seen an up-to-date one, ours being an old model with a gunny sack curtain at the doorway.

"It's not exactly like ours," he explained, "but you just go in and look around and you'll know what to do. You'll see a long chain or string hangin' to it. Before you come out be sure to pull it."

I went in somewhat dubiously. All went well until I pulled the string. Then it sounded as if an avalanche was coming right down on top of my head. Papa had not prepared me for this. I rushed out of there, wild-eyed, yelling at the top of my voice, "Papa, I broke it all to pieces. Don't you hear it?"

"That's all right, honey," he laughed. "They always sound like a combination earthquake and tornado. But what's that you got in your hand?" I looked. It was my drawers.

"Go right back in there an' put 'em on," he said.

"No, sir, I'll never go back in that place. I'm scared of it."

I started walking toward a big tree in the back yard. "I'll hide behind this tree and put them on."

"All right," he smiled, "just so you get 'em on. I'm takin' no lady to see *Macbeth* that ain't wearin' her drawers."

Papa bought a lot of things for that day, but what I liked most was *A Child's Garden of Verses*. The pretty clerk in the store selected the book for him.

That night in starry-eyed amazement I watched the Queen try to wipe imaginary blood from her hands. It must have been the inspiration I got then that made me say to Papa the next day when we were on the train going home, "Papa, I want to be an actress."

"Like hell you do!" he exploded. "Danged if I won't shoot you first!"

The Sawmill Changes Hands

ONE NIGHT Papa came home from the mill apparently in a disturbed state of mind.

When Mama met him at the door he didn't say, "Hello, honey," as usual. Instead he walked across the room and hung his hat on the wall peg, then turned and said abruptly, "I'm afraid there's something in the wind. Two fellows been hangin' 'round the office all day. I think they want to buy the mill." Papa had just been made overall manager of the Middlebrook Lumber Company and the thought of the mill going into other hands was not a happy one for him.

The mysterious men returned the following day and conferred with Mr. Middlebrook for several hours. A few days later Papa's suspicions were confirmed. They bought the mill, paying Mr. Middlebrook fifteen thousand dollars cash and obligating themselves to pay fifteen thousand more in annual installments of five thousand dollars. Papa learned these details when he was called in to sign papers relating to the sale. He learned, also, the identity of the buyers, who were Mr. Joe A. Bentley and Mr. Ed Zimmerman. After taking over the management of their new enterprise, the owners assured Papa that he would be retained in his job, as would all other employees.

Joe Bentley and Ed Zimmerman were both young bachelors. They were about Papa's age, and it was not long before the trio formed a close friendship which was to last throughout their lifetime. Papa's association with what later became known as the fabulous J. A. Bentley Lumber Company was unique and probably unparalleled in employer-employee relationship. Many interesting and amusing incidents grew out of it. Neither of the bachelors ever married.

Years later when Joe and Ed became multimillionaires and Papa's friends spoke to him about them somewhat critically, he defended them. Knowing that Papa's faithfulness and ingenuity had done much to promote the amassing of their vast fortune, his friends would ask, "Why ain't you never insisted on a partnership?" Papa would reply, "Oh, they offered me a partnership long time ago, but I didn't want it." Then he'd take a puff or two on his old pipe and add, "I reckon I had about all I needed most of my life. And I reckon I ain't stayed awake nights like Joe and Ed worryin' about somebody stealin' it from me."

Aunt [68] *Puss*

During the years while Papa worked for Mr. Middlebrook he saved from his earnings one thousand dollars, which he deposited in a Beaumont bank. This money contributed its part to the success of the J. A. Bentley Lumber Company. A year after Joe and Ed bought the mill their note came due and they didn't have enough cash to meet it. Papa knew about their plight, so he said, "I got a thousand in the bank—you can have it." They borrowed Papa's money then and every year after until their note was cancelled. They would give it back to him in monthly payments, and then at the end of the year it was ready to borrow again.

When they paid Papa, after their note was cancelled, and told him they would not need it again, Papa chuckled, "Well, bully for that. You've dang near wore it out."

Papa was repaid in many ways for his devotion to Joe and Ed. Ed, who died four months before Papa, did remember him in his will. During the latter years of Papa's life Joe and Ed never let him work in the forest alone. They sent a younger man along to look after him. Papa growled about it at times, "I don't want that wet nurse followin' me 'round. I'm seveny years old and dang well able to take care of myself." But the young man continued to stay as close to him as his shadow.

Spurger Crossing

Aunt Puss

We Move to Louisiana

FEW THINGS in this life are static. And so our years at Plank came to an end when I was eleven years old.

The timber supply for the mill was exhausted. The owners had to look for another pine forest. The two bachelors were no longer short of money; their initial investment of thirty thousand dollars had paid off well, and they could buy anything they wanted and pay cash for it. Papa was sent to central Louisiana on a scouting trip.

"Look for timbered land and a good location for a sawmill. Then, when you find 'em, buy 'em," Joe and Ed told him.

We'd heard so much about Louisiana swamps, mosquitoes, and alligators that we kissed Papa goodbye with apprehension and noisy grief. Even Mama's usual calm was broken by poorly concealed sobs. We thought we'd never see him again. "Never, never," wailed Aunt Puss, who had come to attend what was more like a funeral service than a going-away party. But to our joy and surprise Papa returned after a few weeks, hale and hearty. And he didn't bring back with him the sign of a single mosquito bite.

His official report pleased Joe and Ed so much that they left immediately for Louisiana to close a deal and pay for their first tract of land in Louisiana, the virgin pine forest that was to start them on their way to great wealth.

After they left, things began to move in a hurry. The mill was dismantled and the machinery packed into boxcars that stood on a railroad siding. In a few days an engine backed up to the cars, pulled them out onto the main track and we watched them roll away. Plank soon was to become a ghost town, because the day after the boxcars were carried off with the inanimate part of what had been Plank's backbone

Aunt [70] *Puss*

nailed down inside them, Papa left overland with our little town's heart—the men and the oxen. Their trip to Louisiana was clouded by only one tragedy. Old Rawbones, Papa's favorite ox, was hurt while fording the Sabine River. He had to be shot and left behind.

When the boxcars reached their destination in Louisiana, which was not then even a whistle stop on the Texas and Pacific Railroad eighteen miles north of Alexandria, the machinery was reassembled and the mill set up beside a big "pond," which was a body of water that had been left with no outlet when Red River cut its course through new territory. The new town was named Zimmerman in honor of Ed. Houses sprang up almost overnight, and people moved into them and changed them from houses into homes.

Soon the hum of a circular saw could be heard from six a.m. to six p.m., and the noise of the shrill whistle of the "dinky" that hauled logs in from the forest could be heard above that of lumber being stacked to dry in the lumberyards.

In due time Mama and her five children arrived on the scene. On our way from Texas the train made a short stop at Lafayette, Louisiana. There I saw my first pushcart full of ripe bananas. The vendors pushed carts alongside the coaches and sold the fruit to the passengers, delivering it through the screenless windows. Bananas, hundreds of bananas, right there before our eyes! Yes, surely, we were going to like Louisiana. Swamps, mosquitoes, and alligators—how could we worry about such things when for the first time in our lives we all had our fill of bananas, and for the amazingly low price of one nickel? From Lafayette we went to Alexandria on the H.E. & W.T. Railroad. They called it "Hell Either Way you Take it." When we arrived at Zimmerman we found Papa at the depot. He welcomed us joyously, and proudly introduced Mama to his friends when we met them as we walked home.

Aunt [71] *Puss*

Our back yard bordered the "pond," which had a steep bank and overhanging trees that were covered with Spanish moss. As soon as possible, after Papa led us into the house, set down our "telescope-luggage," and said, "This is your home," I slipped out the back door and, under the glow of the setting sun, sat down to begin my lookout for an alligator. Papa coaxed me inside the house just as dark blacked out my view.

I Fall in Love

WE LIVED at Zimmerman only two years, but many things happened while we were there. I fell in love for the first time. I was twelve then, and the object of my affections was fourteen. The Zimmermans, distantly related to Ed, came down from Manistee, Michigan, and moved into a home just across the paling fence from us.

Up to that time boys had meant little to me. They were just nuisances always looking for an opportunity to give my pigtails a jerk or a twist. Nor did the Zimmerman family mean anything to me. No, not until I saw Don, my first love. He was the same Don Zimmerman who later distinguished himself as a baseball player, the same Don whose son, Don, Jr., distinguished himself with Tulane's "Green Wave."

Every time Don glanced across the paling fence my heart skipped a beat. I sat for hours on our front porch just waiting for him to pass and say, "Good evening." When school opened in September and Don chose me from among all the others to be his girl, my heart all but failed from too much joy.

The most embarrassing thing I can remember happened

Aunt [72] *Puss*

once following a blizzard which left Zimmerman ice-bound and shivering. One of my home duties was to carry out the chamber pot every morning and empty it in our Chick Sale. On this particular morning I picked it up and started jauntily down the back steps, then on down the plank walk that led to where I was going. I heard Mama call, "Emmy, you'll slip and break your neck if you're not careful." I paid little attention to her warning. Walking more jauntily than ever, I tripped along humming a tune. I was in love and full of music. I became too happily careless, and then it happened.

Just before I reached the door of the little outhouse my feet slipped from under me and I sat down hard on the ice-coated walk. At the same time the chamber pot sat down hard, too, on its bottom, splashing its contents all over my face and hair.

Don was the first thought that came to me. I hoped he wasn't looking out his window. Clumsily, I crawled to my feet, then slyly glanced across the paling fence. Yes, there he was right on his walk looking at me. He was carrying a chamber pot too. He turned his head aside quickly, not wanting me to know he'd witnessed my humiliation. I blessed him for doing this. Don, my first love, was a gentleman.

Don and his family did not stay at Zimmerman long. His going left me lonely and desolate. After leaving he wrote me three letters, which I kept for many years. Then other interests came to both of us and he passed forever from my life.

Aunt [73] *Puss*

Emma Wilson (Emery) at 17

Aunt [74] *Puss*

Joe's Horseless Carriage

PAPA and his boss, Joe Bentley, who was also his best friend, had some arguments while we lived at Zimmerman. That was after Joe got his horseless carriage. It was the first automobile seen in that part of the country, and no one but Joe liked it. The farmers swore at it when it frightened their horses and made them run away, spilling bales of cotton and hay along the roadside, and sometimes throwing people from the wagon seat, causing them to be injured. Papa used to tell Joe, "The danged thing may run on level ground, but it'll never make the hills."

"Oh, yes, she will," Joe would argue. "I'll bet you fifty dollars she will." Once after I heard Joe say that, I saw Papa show Mama a fifty dollar check he'd collected on Joe's bet.

A pair of mules pulled Joe and his automobile up many a hill. In fact, he kept a man and a pair of mules cached away at convenient places in the hills for that purpose, and a man always rode with him in the automobile, one who could get out and walk the hills to bring back the mules when they were needed.

Joe often stopped by our house to pick me up and take me with him when he saw me playing in our yard. He'd put on the brakes suddenly and yell, "Emmy, want t' go ridin'?" I'd climb in beside him and shout back, "I'm gone, Mama!" In a minute we'd be out of sight. Papa didn't like Joe's picking me up for a ride, and he told him so. "You're goin' to kill my young'un yet in that danged thing."

Joe'd smile and say, "Say nothing more about it, Henry. Emmy likes to feel her hair standing out in the wind when we race downhill."

And I did like it, that is, until one day when Joe and I

and his pride and joy all piled up in the dry bed of Seiper Creek. Neither Joe nor I suffered internal injuries, but Joe's automobile had so many she had to be junked. I was skinned in spots from end to end. Joe took me to a doctor and had me bandaged before Papa saw me. After Papa's first shock on looking at me had passed, he turned to Joe and said, "Dang it all. I told you so."

Papa Plants His Family in the Wilderness

WHEN I was thirteen we left Zimmerman and moved into a little four-room house that was eighteen miles deep in a Louisiana virgin pine forest. Some woodsmen, who were helping Papa survey the Company's land, built it for him.

Our entire family had fallen victims of malaria, so Papa said to Joe, "It looks like my whole family will die of that stuff if I don't get 'em away from this millpond and the mosquitoes."

Our new home was two miles beyond the end of the narrow-gauge dinky track over which the logs were hauled to the mill. Despite its isolation we thought it the most beautiful place in the world. The longleaf pines reached high toward the sky, and beneath them in springtime grew a carpet of wild violets, purple and white. In the bottoms, along the banks of little creeks that sang gaily and, sometimes after heavy rains shouted wildly, native flowers bloomed in great profusion. No bottled perfume from Paris could ever duplicate the fragrance that filled the air when they waved their shell-pink blossoms in the breeze.

This forest where I spent most of my youth, and which I

grew to love with a depth of feeling I have never been able to express with words, holds a singularly cherished place in my memory. It was here that I received my higher education from the wild birds and animals and the pines that almost spoke a human language.

Here, in the forest, was the shy little fawn that ate out of my hand, meeting me at the same place every day to get her dinner; the robin that became such a good friend and often sat on my shoulder and plucked at my hair; and the little beaver who looked up from his work long enough to say with his eyes, "You're welcome, stay as long as you like."

It was in this forest, too, that I became well acquainted with my parents. We grew close to one another in a way that would have been impossible had we lived in the noise and confusion of a world outside this quiet place.

To this forest Aunt Puss once came to visit us, "her kinfolks." One day while she was there she said, "Henry, it don't make no difference if Emmy gets lonesome livin' in th' woods. She'll get more learnin' from all God's miles of nature than she'd get from any of them schools in big cities." Papa sat quietly and did not answer.

It was over a period of several years in these rolling hills that Papa surveyed and estimated many hundreds of acres of land and trees. Sometimes when he was at work I walked with him mile on mile helping carry his steel tapeline and other equipment. At times we rode our small but rugged ponies.

When Papa's helper "Flop," a big good-natured backwoodsman, started out early in the morning to saddle two of the ponies for the day's work, he would look at Papa and say, "Which hoss y'u fetchin' t'day?" Papa would go on lacing his shoes as he yawned back at him, "Whichever one that ain't asleep."

Papa gave Flop his nickname because all too often during work hours he'd seen him stretch himself out on the ground and say, "Lemme flop here jes a minute in th' shade an' ketch my wind."

Sometimes Papa would say, "Flop, you can stay home today and work the pea patch. I'll take Emmy along to help me."

Papa loved the trees. He often spoke to them as if they were living people. He'd point to a big pine and say, "He's been here a long time, much longer than I have and he'll be here long after I'm gone." Then, in, an undertone, he'd add more to himself than to me, "If some danged fool don't cut him down."

Sometimes he'd put his ear to the ground and listen a minute, then get up and say, "She ain't talkin' today, she's plumb silent."

Pine–shake roof

Aunt [78] *Puss*

My Fortune in Boyce

IT WAS EARLY in the morning on my fourteenth birthday when Papa said, "Emmy, run along and jump into your Sunday dress. I'll take you to Boyce with me for your birthday present."

I ran along and quicker than a wink slid into my pink and white gingham. It was plaid, made with a bolero of solid pink. My pride was the hidden pocket on the lower left facing of the jacket.

When we started to climb into the buggy to drive to town eighteen miles away, Papa, who also knew about the secret pocket, leaned over and slipped a silver dollar into it, saying as he did so, "While I'm tradin' and tendin' to business you can look around and find somethin' to buy for yourself." Perhaps he never would have given me the dollar had he known how I'd spend it.

When we reached Boyce it was eleven o'clock. After we'd eaten our lunch, which we called "dinner," at a small restaurant, Papa left me standing outside gazing into a store window. As he started through the doorway to go into the bank building he said to me, "Meet me right here in an hour."

I felt gay and happy and rich as I fingered the dollar in my pocket. I was trying to decide what to buy with it, so I started walking up and down the street looking into store windows. I had already decided to spend half of it on a present for Mama.

I had not looked very long before I saw just the thing for her. It was a black spittoon with red roses painted on it in a festooned design that encircled it. I'd heard her get after Flop, our man of all work, a lot of times about where he spat his tobacco juice, so I thought this spittoon was bound to improve his habit and at the same time please Mama because with the roses on it it was a work of art.

When the clerk put it in a plain brown paper bag, I looked at him pleadingly and said, "It's a present, please tie it up in white paper." He smiled indulgently, and from behind the counter drew out some coarse yellow paper and wrapped the package carefully.

"This is the best paper I have," he apologized as he handed me the package.

With the black spittoon under my arm I walked out proudly, and started down the street. I had not gone far when I saw a two-story, white house with a sign painted on the front which read "City Hotel." A smaller sign was nailed to one of the gallery posts saying, "Your Palm Read For Fifty Cents."

My heart began to flutter—maybe I could have my fortune told! I stood there a minute, tightening my arm on the spittoon, remembering that I'd heard Papa say, "Fortune telling is of the devil's making." I knew he'd skin me alive if I went into that house. But oh how I wanted to do it!

The temptation was too great, so I walked right into the yard, up the steps and on into the hallway. One of the doors that led into a room was half open. I peeped in. A very dark-complexioned man sat there reading a book.

I was about to retreat in panic, but before I could do so he saw me and said in a kindly voice, "Little one, can I do something for you?" I almost swallowed my tongue as I nodded my head in the affirmative. He pointed to a chair beside a table. I went over and sat on the edge of it.

In the center of the table there was a large crystal ball. I was still holding Mama's present tightly. The man sat down down in a chair opposite me and reached out for my hand. I gave it to him and he laid it on the table, palm up, then bent over and gazed at it intently.

In a moment he rose suddenly, walked to the door of an

Aunt [80] *Puss*

adjoining room and called, "Yoleka, come, please." A beautiful young woman, as dark as he, wearing some kind of oriental robe, appeared in the doorway. He said to her in an undertone which I could not have heard had not my ears been tuned to the rhythm of my nerves, "Look at this child's hand. It's amazing."

The dark woman walked over and picked up my hand, which, in my half-dazed condition, I had not closed nor lifted from the table. After studying it briefly, she said to the man, "Yes, it is amazing. There are few like it." After that she went back into the other room. The man sat down again and studied my palm. By this time I had found my voice, and in a timid manner I asked, "Mister, will anything ever happen to me?"

I remember few of the things the East Indian told me that day, but I do remember how he answered that question. "No, no, my child," he said. "Things will never happen to you. They won't have time. You'll happen to them first."

He patted me on the shoulder and smiled when I gave him my fifty cents.

I looked in every direction as I walked out through the gateway and on to the sidewalk. I was afraid I'd happen to something any minute.

Before I'd gone a block I saw Papa and a big man hurrying toward me. The man was wearing a pistol in a holster on his hip. I could tell that Papa was upset and the man was trying to reason with him. I knew, from his looks and that formidable weapon hanging at his side, that the man must be the town constable.

"Where on earth you been, Emmy? I been scared out of my wits."

I knew I dared not tell him the truth right then; I'd save it until he was more calm.

I said, "Oh, I've been looking at Red River from the bridge. See it, Papa, the river runs right over there."

Aunt [81] *Puss*

"Yes, young lady, I know very well where the river is," he all but shouted at me. "It's been running under that bridge for quite a while."

After his scare began to wear off he put his arm around me and said, "Emmy, danged if I ain't glad I found you. You 'bout scared the blue blazes out of me." Then he turned and shook hands with the man and said, "Thank you, constable, for helpin' me, and goodbye, we'll be goin' now."

On the way home I argued with my conscience. Papa and I were very close. I'd never kept a secret from him and I knew that sooner or later I'd tell him about the fortuneteller. But I was afraid there'd be an explosion when I did.

It was nearly dark and we were almost home before I decided to cast the die. Papa was in a calm mood and lost in his own thoughts when I blurted out, "Papa, I had my fortune told today. It cost me fifty cents." He tightened his grip on the reins, clucked at the horses, and kept looking straight ahead.

I steadied my shoulders against the potential storm, but it didn't come. Instead, he mumbled absent-mindedly, "Your fortune told? Well I'll be danged." Then, much to my surprise, he slid back into his own channel of thinking.

Looking at him out of the corner of my eye I realized that he had not caught the import of what I said. My confession had not punctured the concentration of his own thoughts. But, at least, I'd tried and my conscience would not reproach me again.

I Try Teaching

THERE WERE a few natives who lived in the forest where we were. Very few of them could read or write. One day a man forty years old said to Papa, "Mr. Wilson, do you think your daughter, Miss Emmy, would teach some of us an' our chillern how to read and and write an' figger? We'd pay her if she would."

"She might teach you how to read and write," Papa said, "but as to figurin', she don't know much about that herself. She's only a child, you know." Then he went on, "I'll ask her and if she'll try it I'll furnish the lumber to build a little schoolhouse."

In a few weeks the new schoolhouse opened its doors to all comers, and I took my seat at a little homemade table to begin what was to be my abbreviated career as a teacher.

Fifteen pupils, who ranged in ages from ten to forty years, were to pay me one dollar a month for my services. To me that seemed a big fee when compared to the ten cents a week Papa paid me for looking after his baths.

I took my work seriously and so did my pupils. They were there for one purpose only, to learn how to read and write. After everything was running smoothly Papa decided that my three brothers, whose ages were seven, nine, and thirteen, should join the classes. They did so reluctantly, and in a few days I saw the handwriting on the wall. I suppose I should more correctly say, I saw the chair on the rafters.

My brothers thought it a great big joke that I should try to teach them something. After all, hadn't they taught me how to shin a tree, dig fish bait, and fish up doodlebugs by spitting on the end of a broom straw, then dropping the spit-on end down in a tiny hole in the ground where the doodlebug lived?

Yes, they glanced at one another and winked knowingly when I started telling them how to do things. They could not quite digest me as a dignified schoolma'am. I could not make myself tell Papa how they were acting because I knew he'd trim them to within an inch of their lives if I did.

The blow fell on a bright, sunny Tuesday at high noon. I went with the girls to a shady spot on the bank of Seiper

Aunt [83] *Puss*

Creek not far from the schoolhouse where we usually ate our lunches. At the proper time we went back to the schoolroom and I rang the bell. Everyone, including my brothers, hurried in and took their seats on the benches.

When I started to sit down at my table desk I saw that my chair was missing. I looked about the room, but it was not in sight. About that time I heard a bit of giggling which came from the corner where my blood kin sat.

Presently a dignified man who seemed to be embarrassed, said, "Miss Emmy, your brother tied it up there."

My eyes followed his finger as he pointed upward. And, sure enough, there it was, my chair tied to the rafter with a rope. I had been prepared for almost anything, so I took this in my stride. I spoke to Bolton since he was the oldest. "Bolton, get it down, please," I said. He looked obstinate as he replied, "I don't want to and I won't."

Nothing I said after that changed his mind. He was a lot bigger than I, but I was undaunted.

"Go, please, and bring me a big switch," I said to the man who had pointed out the chair to me.

Hurriedly, he went out through the open doorway and returned in less than three minutes with a whopper.

By this time I could see that some of the grown-up men there wanted to take things into their own hands. But I begged, "Please let me do this in my own way. I can do it, you watch and see." They watched and they saw.

By this time Bolton looked somewhat apprehensive, and my other brothers seemed worried.

After the man gave me the switch I walked over to where Bolton sat on the bench and demanded in a low voice, "You take down my chair." I realized that a lot depended on his reaction to my command.

"No," he said, "I will not."

"All right," I told him, "I'm going to switch you so Papa won't have to do it tonight."

Aunt [84] *Puss*

I'd never struck anything in my life, so I shut my eyes when I raised the switch. Then I felt Bolton rush past me like a gust of wind. When I opened my eyes I saw him jumping through the open window near my table at the back of the room. I was so struck with fury that I threw dignity and discretion aside. Before I had time to catch up with my shattered poise I dashed after him and jumped through the same window where he had made his hurried exit.

He had gained some ground on me, but I could run fast, and in a minute I knew that I would soon overtake him. He was running fast too, and looking back at me now and then without slackening his speed.

By the time he reached the creek I was only an arm's length behind him. He ran on to the big foot log that bridged the stream. I threw down my switch and followed him. In the middle of the span I grabbed him. We tussled for a moment above the water, which was deep and cold, and then both of us fell in headfirst.

Bolton was a good swimmer, but I couldn't swim a stroke. For a moment I struggled for breath, and then lost all sense of what was going on. The next thing I knew I was lying on the ground where Bolton had dragged me out of the water, and he was trying to beat some life into me.

As soon as I caught my breath Bolton stood up, his wet clothes clinging to him. He was silent for a little while. Then he bent down and picked up my switch. Tears were running down his face, and offering the switch to me, he said, "Emmy, get up right now and beat the devil out of me."

After a while we started home, two sorry-looking objects. Just before we reached the gate, Bolton looked at me and said, "I'm going out and cut down some big trees and sell 'em and make some money and buy you a gold bracelet with your name carved on it."

Aunt [85] *Puss*

Mama and the Burglars

DESPITE the etheral quality that often manifested itself in Mama's personality, there was also a very practical, human side. She was afraid of certain things, one of them being a burglar.

She owned piteously little that could have attracted the attention of a burglar, but she felt certain that one would eventually break into our house and carry away her six silver spoons, which she kept hidden between the mattresses on her bed, or he just might haul off her beloved organ. She could not quite hide that away because it was big and heavy, the kind you had to pump full of air with your feet before it would make music.

Papa was often away from home. At such times Mama would worry about the considerable sums of money he kept in the house. On the first day of every month he paid the workmen at "The Front." These were the men who cut down the trees, sawed them into certain lengths, then loaded the logs on flatcars. These flats were drawn by the dinky over a narrow-gauge railroad to the sawmill at Zimmerman.

Papa often brought the money from the office at the mill a day or so before payday. When he did so he hid it in an old trunk under his bed. A good many people were familiar with his routine and this gave Mama a lot of anxiety, especially if Papa was called away while the money was in the trunk.

Once Papa said, "Eula, I must teach you how to shoot a gun so you won't be afraid when I'm away from home." But Mama didn't want to shoot any gun. "I'm more afraid of guns that I am of burglars," she declared.

Despite Mama's protest, Papa came in one day with two shiny new pistols and laid them on Mama's bedroom mantel,

Aunt [86] *Puss*

high above the fireplace where curious little boys couldn't reach them. He winked at me and whispered, "I'll just lay 'em here in full view so she can get used to 'em." Then about once a week he'd say to Mama, "Eula, let's go on a shooting party. I want you to learn to take a pistol in each hand and shoot 'em both at the same time." But Mama never was quite ready.

"I'm too busy today," was always her excuse. So the pistols continued to decorate the mantel along with a framed photograph of George Washington.

They say if you look for a thing long enough you'll surely find it, and so it was with Mama's burglar. The only difference was that Mama expected only one but they came in duplicate.

It happened late on a moonlit night when the money was in the house and Papa was twenty miles from home.

Even the owls had hushed their screeching and gone to bed. I was asleep on my little cot in the lean-to which opened into Mama's bedroom. Bolton was asleep near me on another bed. To this day when I look back at the happenings of that night I feel a shivery sensation moving up and down my spine.

The first I knew about the awful thing swooping down on us was when Mama shook me out of my sound sleep.

A shaft of moonlight was lying across my cot. After I sat up and rubbed the sleep out of my eyes, I saw Mama standing in its glow. In each hand she was holding a shiny new pistol.

Presently she leaned over me and whispered, "There's two burglars hidden outside in the shadow of the chimney."

I began to shake all over.

"They waked me up, talking low," she declared. "I saw them through the window."

My heart jumped right up into my throat and began choking me. With Papa gone, two burglars just outside the window, nearly a thousand dollars in the old trunk under the bed, and Mama pointing two pistols straight at my head, my teeth started chattering. It was too much for a fourteen-year-old to take with equanimity.

I crawled off my cot, grabbed the chamber pot, which fortunately was still empty, turned it upside down and sat on it so I could shiver better.

Mama never was one to delay action if a thing had to be done. After she was sure that I was wide awake she went to Bolton's bed and began to shake him. In a minute he sat up, rubbing his eyes just as I had done.

"I want you to yell something real loud and sudden," Mama whispered to him—Bolton had just reached the age when his voice was changing. "For mercy's sake," Mama added, "don't yell like a little boy. Use your man's voice this time." Then to my horror Mama said, "When you yell out loud and coarse I'm going to shoot both pistols right at the spot where they're standing."

Frightened half to death, Bolton kept murmuring, "Yes, Mama; yes, Mama; yes, Mama!"

"Say it like your papa would," she instructed. "Say, I hate to kill a man but I'm fixin' to blow you to pieces. Say it loud as you can."

By this time I was shivering so violently the chamber pot was remaining under me with difficulty.

I started to stop my ears with my fingers, then hesitated because even while I was quaking inside I was curious to hear which of Bolton's voices would come out when he opened his mouth.

Then it happened. Bolton let go his warning in a clear lyric soprano. Mama waited for him to finish; then she let go two blasts with her twin pistols that sounded like the end of the world as they shattered the stillness of the night and a glass window near the fireplace.

After a moment's deadly silence we heard a man groan,

"I'm shot." Then silence again. Presently Mama tiptoed over to peep out through the shattered window. She saw two men hurrying away, one supporting the other.

The next morning we found a trail of dark blood that lay like a ribbon across the white sand in the yard.

When Papa returned late in the afternoon, Bolton and I both tried to tell him the story at the same time. When we'd finished he chuckled, "And so your ma shot both pistols at once? Danged if I ain't proud of her."

Old Bragg—Saratoga Road

Aunt Puss

More About Papa

PAPA was the axis around which my life revolved. Although others could seldom sway him after he'd set his mind to a thing, I could wheedle him out of anything.

I remember once when we lived in the deep forest, I said to him abruptly, "Papa, I want a sidesaddle so I can ride in to the mill."

Very emphatically, Papa replied, "No! You got no business with a sidesaddle. You put one of them things on Gyp and she'll throw you sky high." I wilted, but only temporarily, and he knew it. Then he warned me, "Young lady, I want no shenanigans about this. Let's just bury the question."

Outwardly I was subdued, but inwardly I had no idea of burying the question. I'd been riding Gyp too long with only a blanket thrown across her back.

I think our two ponies must have been twins. They were almost identical. One day Papa had come home with two strange ponies. He was riding one of them and leading the other. He handed me the reins of the one he was riding, saying "This one is yours; her name is Gyp. This other one is mine; her name is Jap."

From this time on for several years, we rode our ponies together in and out of the forest, and it is this picture of him that I have kept in my mind and heart: Papa on his little sorrel pony under the tall pines.

I waited awhile and then decided it was safe to disinter the question of the sidesaddle. After about a half dozen attacks on a defenseless man (he didn't believe in striking a woman), I looked out the window one day and saw Papa rolling up the narrow-gauge dinky track that ran in front of our cabin. Strapped to the rear seat of his velocipede was an odd-looking object which had something dangling on the right side. On investigation I learned that the dangling appendage was the stirrup on my sidesaddle.

Since I had been successful in this skirmish I soon tried another. This time I attacked while his bars were down. I'd learned that a sudden swift punch was best. Hugging his neck and kissing his forehead, I waited until he was all but choked, then let him have it. "Papa, I want a big trunk with a tray and a lock and key. I want . . ." Before I could get in any more he whispered through his aching throat, "You got nothin' to put in a trunk."

I squeezed his throat tighter and hushed him up. Then I continued, "I want to lock up my diary so my brothers can't find it." By this time he'd pushed me off his lap and regained his equilibrium. "You got no business keeping secrets from your brothers," he said.

The trunk came easier than the sidesaddle. Not long after the first attack it arrived on the rear seat of the velocipede. The day he put it in my room and handed me the key, I had a woman-to-woman talk with Mama. It was almost bedtime when I kissed her and said, "Mama, aren't fathers wonderful!" Mama's answer was then above my head but later I realized what she meant when she smiled and said, "Yes, they are wonderful. And they're completely helpless, too, when they land in the clutches of a diplomat."

Papa's Baths

NOT SINCE Cleopatra's handmaidens washed her luxuriously oiled body in the waters of the Nile has there been anything more interesting in the way of baths than Papa's semiweekly scrubs while we were in the forest.

Aunt [91] *Puss*

He used to say, "Some folks think one bath a week is plenty, but not for me. I'm takin' two if it dries up the well." He'd glance at me to see if I approved, because I was his water carrier. I'd smile at him, then he'd go on, "Yes, siree, I'd hate to look a skunk in the face if I didn't bathe mor'n once a week."

Every Saturday night Papa paid me twenty cents for looking after his baths. It was the first money I ever earned and I was proud of it.

Winter was always the hardest on me. I'd drag in the heavy cypress washtub on Wednesdays and Saturdays, set it down in the kitchen near the cookstove. Then after we'd finished supper, I'd chuck up the fire and fill a bucket and all the pans I could find with water, put them on the stove, and start heating it. When it was scalding hot, I'd pour it into the tub and add enough cold water from the well to make it just right. After placing a towel and a bar of soap on a chair near the tub, I'd ring a little sheep bell we kept on a shelf in the kitchen. Presently Papa would come rushing through the open ice-cold hallway to the warm kitchen and take his bath.

In summer we had a different routine, and it was much easier on my back. I'd drag the old tub off its bench in the back yard, set it near the bored well where the sun could shine on it, then fill it with water. By the time Papa was ready to use it just after dark, it was exactly the right temperature.

It was summer time and in the dark of the moon when something happened that just about put an end to Papa's open-air bathing. I suppose it never would have happened if on that day I had not set the tub too close to the fence, and the fence had not been covered with a dense growth of vines that were loaded with ripe dewberries. But how was I to know that the king of all snakes was going to have his evening meal there on that very day?

Aunt [92] *Puss*

That night Papa went out as usual and crawled into his bath. Mama had gone to bed. I was sitting in a chair near the table in her room reading *Little Women* by the light of a kerosene lamp. Suddenly I heard something out in the back yard that sounded like a Comanche yell. Then, swift as the wind and roaring like a freshet, it burst into the house.

The strange sound had been Papa in flight.

The next thing I knew he was standing between the foot of Mama's bed and my chair. He was completely nude, and he was wrestling with a long snake who seemed to be enjoying the encounter much more than his opponent. Apparently there was nothing vicious about the reptile. He seemed to be in a playful mood.

I sat spellbound watching the fight while Mama sat upright in bed clutching the sheet.

After Papa freed himself and the snake slithered gracefully across the room and out the doorway, Mama and I looked at each other a bit guiltily because neither of us had offered Papa any heroic gesture of assistance. By this time he had grabbed the sheet from Mama and wrapped it about himself. He was breathing hard when he sat down in a rocker and said, "Danged if the sunovasquirt didn't crawl right in the tub with me. Thought I could shake him off in the yard, but time I loosed him from my leg he'd grab my arm."

Papa was swaying back and forth in his rocker and talking jerkily. "Then I thought about the light in the house, maybe that would scare him, but no, not him—he wanted to play games."

Mama and I still were mute and shaky, too, as Papa rose from his chair. He hadn't yet seen any humor in the episode as he said, "I guess tomorrow he'll expect me to have a lantern hangin' on the fence so he can pick his dewberries easier."

Aunt [93] *Puss*

Papa and Music

I WAS PROUD of the way Papa could play the fiddle. His was not a Stradivarius, but he could make it laugh and cry when he wanted to. He liked to dance, too.

Mama never went with him when he attended the dances. Along with many other ideas which she had absorbed from her God-fearing father was the firm belief that those who indulged in dancing and card playing never got any closer to heaven than a brief peep through a crack in the Pearly Gates when they were being opened to let someone else in. I can't remember ever seeing a deck of cards in our house.

Papa liked nothing better than a game of poker. His pokering habits caused Mama grave anxiety. She seldom rebuked him with words, but her soft gray eyes often reflected her concern over the ultimate safety of his soul.

I was thirteen when he began taking me with him to all the backwoods shindigs. His decision to do this gave Mama two souls to worry about instead of one. At first she raised a protest, but in the end gave her consent. Although she never said so, I suspect she decided that if Papa must go it might be well for him to have a chaperon. During the four years between my thirteenth and seventeenth birthdays I shared most of his social activities.

When I was fourteen Papa hired Mr. Peavy, a young redhead with a brand-new certificate from the State Teachers' College at Natchitoches, to come out and live with us and teach me and the younger children. I learned a lot from Mr. Peavy; too much, Papa decided when to our curriculum was added the art of romance. My education under the guidance of Mr. Peavy ended suddenly after Papa learned he'd asked to marry me. I cried when my true love left, but it was not long before romance again crossed my path. I'll say no more about my youthful affairs of the heart.

Aunt [94] *Puss*

Good-bye, Aunt Puss

IT WAS APRIL in Spurger. Sunlight flooded the little community. There things always started happening early in the morning. Up at the blacksmith shop Clem Cotten went about his job of shoeing horses while Sim Carter passed the time o'day with his customers at the general store.

Uncle Lum sat erect in the surrey as he slowly covered the twenty-three miles between his home and the courthouse at Woodville, the county seat. He was on his way to have some legal papers signed.

Uncle Lum was happy. He had just sold forty acres of his timbered land, and he expected to bring back to Aunt Puss two hundred dollars to put in the milk crock where she kept their savings. Uncle Lum rarely whistled, but today his clear notes echoed through the forest like the voice of a whippoorwill.

Outside Aunt Puss's kitchen window a mockingbird sang gaily in the big elm tree. Aunt Puss faced this day as, all her life, she had faced her days, with peace and contentment in her heart. "You young'uns make haste now an' get off to school," she urged. "You-all are the only two I got left at home an' I want you should get a eggucation like your pa." She kept talking as she buttoned up Johnnie's shirt and ran a comb through his blond, wiry hair. "I want you-all to be able to read them books Mr. Shakespeare wrote, read 'em an' know what he's talkin' about."

In a little while the boys were gone and the house was quiet. Now Aunt Puss began setting the place in order. She tidied the kitchen and left it clean and shiny like a newly polished winesap apple, and it smelled just as fragrant. Presently she went to the front room and turned her attention to Uncle Lum's books that lay on a table near the fireplace. "I must dust 'em," she thought.

Aunt [95] *Puss*

Picking up his volume of *Hamlet,* she studied the binding seriously. "H-A-M-L-E-T," she spelled the name out letter by letter, then pronounced it slowly, "Hamlet." "Well, I'm thankful, at least I can read. Some pore creatures can't even do that." She still held the book and gazed at the letters on the binding, "Yes, Mr. Shakespeare," she murmured, "I want my young'uns to know what you're talkin' about when they read your books. I wisht I knowed," she said sadly, "but I don't."

In a little while Lottie Hooks drove up to the front gate in her buggy. She got out, tied her horse to the hitching post and came into the house. Lottie was Oscar Hook's wife— that made her Aunt Puss's daughter-in-law. Aunt Puss greeted Lottie warmly with a hug and kiss, then asked, "Lottie, what's that you got in your han's?"

"Oh, it's jest a dish of pertato salad I fetched fer our dinner. I'm aimin' to spend the day."

"Sure you goin' to spend the day. But that's a mighty big dish of salad for two wimin to eat."

"Never you mind, we'll eat it," Lottie laughed. Lottie laid her sunbonnet on the bed and looked about the room. "Puss," she said, "I never seen your house when it didn' look purty and smell sweet. Always a vase of flowers settin' on your dinner table."

Aunt Puss smiled her appreciation. "Yes, I try to make it nice so the young'uns'll want to stay at home. My last two is growin' up, soon they'll be leavin' school," Aunt Puss sighed. "You know what that'll mean, them gettin' married and leavin' home like all the others."

Lottie kept gazing about the room. Presently she said, "Puss, all you need to make your house perfec' is a little canary bird in a cage over there in the corner to sing for you."

"No, Lottie, I couldn' keep nothin' caged, no more'n I'd want somebody to cage me in." Then Aunt Puss added,

Aunt [96] *Puss*

thoughtfully, "I says let the birds and the wild animals run free as air in the woods just like Godamighty aimed 'em to."

"Puss, I guess you're right," Lottie agreed. Lottie sat down, then turned her glance suddenly on Aunt Puss. "I got sompin' to tell you, Puss, that'll make your eyes bulge."

Aunt Puss's eyes halfway bulged right then in surprise because Lottie seldom had anything of interest on her mind to talk about. But now Aunt Puss sensed that Lottie was about to burst with something she'd held in too long. "What is it, Lottie?" she asked.

"Well," Lottie said, "Oscar shore had him a time yestiddy, and the mail didn't get delivered on time either. The train done passed through Hillister and gone 'fore Oscar got there. And he had to leave the mail pouch lay in the Post Office till the train come 'long today."

"What happened to make Oscar late with the mail first time in his life?" Aunt Puss asked.

"Oscar shore couldn' help hisse'f yestiddy," Lottie said. She settled herself more comfortably in her rocker. "Oscar was drivin' by the Pickens' house like he always does. There wasn't nobody in sight but the dog 'cause the ol' man was in the creek field a mile from home burnin' bresh."

Aunt Puss knew that something out of the ordinary was coming up. And she wanted to enjoy it. "Wait a minute, Lottie, and lemme get us a dip o' snuff."

Lottie suddenly sat on the edge of her chair and started rocking back and forth nervously.

Aunt Puss picked up the crockery spittoon and placed it on the floor exactly halfway between their two rockers. She offered the snuff bottle to Lottie. But Lottie said, "I cain't dip and talk both at onct."

Aunt Puss sat down, dug her brush into the snuff bottle, gave it several swift twists, then stuck it into her mouth and said, "Go on, Lottie, go on."

"Well," Lottie said, "just as Oscar was passin' the

Pickens' front gate he heard a woman groanin' inside the house, groanin' loud, awful loud. Then he jumped out of the buggy an' run inside. Never takin' time to hitch his horse." Aunt Puss was now hunched forward in her rocker, listening intently. "An' what you think he saw?"

"What?" Aunt Puss asked excitedly.

"Right there on the bed all by herse'f pore Miz Pickens had done had her baby."

Aunt Puss chuckled, "Lottie, 'scuse me if I 'pear to be laughin'. I ain't raily tickled 'bout pore Miz Pickens. But I'm thinkin' 'bout how Oscar's face must a looked when he saw what he saw." Then seriously, she asked, "What did Oscar do?"

"Well," Lottie said, "Pore Miz Pickens told him to look in her sewin' basket on the center table an' git the scissors, then look in the bureau drawer and git a piece of string. Then she told him to cut the cord 'bout two inches from the baby's navel an' tie it tight with the string."

Lottie sighed and rested a moment, then resumed her story.

"After Oscar done all that she told him to, he put the baby in her arms. Mrs. Pickins said, 'Go fast as you can and git Dr. Mo. Jest havin' a baby ain't all there is to it,' she told Oscar. 'You got to see 'bout the afterbirth too.'"

By now Aunt Puss was greatly concerned. "I'm feared Oscar didn' cut the cord right," she said, "an' if he didn' they'll be trouble."

"I guess he done it right," Lottie said. "I drove out there this mornin' 'fore I come here and they's all right."

There was a sudden noise outside the house. Aunt Puss got up and went to the front door. A dozen women were coming up the front walk, each of them carrying a covered dish or pan in her hands. There were happy greetings all around; then one of them said, "Puss, we brought your birthday dinner. Don't you remember you're sixty today?"

Aunt Puss laughed, "I clean forgot it."

Aunt [98] *Puss*

At noon the women gathered around the dinner table to enjoy the birthday feast. Aunt Puss sat where she could look through the doorway toward the road. Suddenly a shadow crossed her face and she said, "There goes Julie Dawson ridin' to town on that wild horse of hers." She shook her head. "As sure as the sun shines out of the sky that horse'll throw 'er one day and kill 'er."

"Nobody but her pa'd miss 'er much," Lizzie Jordan declared.

"Yes, I'd miss her," Aunt Puss contradicted. "I been prayin' for Julie twenty years ever since she come here with her pa a stranger. She's still a stranger but I'm still prayin' for her. Ever' time she passes my house in her buggy or ridin' her horse, these twenty years, I been askin' Godamighty to put love and understandin' in her heart. I know some day he'll do it."

The women remained silent. There was nothing more they wanted to say about Julie Dawson. At four o'clock Aunt Puss's friends began gathering up their empty pans and dishes. "We got to go 'fore the young'uns come home from school," Sue Jenkins said. "Mine won't know where I'm at."

"My two won't be home 'fore dark," Aunt Puss told them. "They're goin' fishin' with the teacher after school."

"What a good day," Aunt Puss said as she sat down in her rocker on the front gallery. "Such a good birthday, and now so quiet and peaceful, just Godamighty and me here all by ourselves."

Presently Aunt Puss looked down the road toward Spurger. She saw Julie Dawson coming on her big black horse, returning from town. Julie was having trouble. The animal had become frightened by a flock of Aunt Puss's turkeys as they rushed across the road in front of him. He was pawing the air. Julie was remaining on her sidesaddle with difficulty. "Yes, Julie's havin' trouble and it's gettin' worse,"

Aunt Puss murmured. She ran down to the front gate and stood there a minute watching the horse; then she unlatched the gate and ran toward the road. She saw Julie jerk the reins angrily and lash the horse with her whip. After that the animal plunged forward and started galloping wildly. Now he was not only frightened, he was angry.

"I'm goin' to stop him if it kills me," Aunt Puss said under her breath. By now she was standing in the middle of the road, right in the path of the onrushing horse, whose rider was clutching the horn of her saddle for dear life. She had managed somehow to free her foot from the stirrup. Her whip had fallen to the ground.

Aunt Puss stood rigid, awaiting the impact. "I'll grab the reins," she said, "I'll stop him if it kills me. Julie ain't ready to die. She's got to get saved 'fore she dies."

Uncle Lum, returning from Woodville, saw what happened.

In some miraculous manner Julie was able to jump clear of the horse after Aunt Puss had checked his speed with her body.

Julie and Uncle Lum carried Aunt Puss inside the house and laid her on the bed gently. She was conscious and smiling.

"I sure stopped him, didn't I, Lum?"

"Yes, honey, you sure did." Uncle Lum smiled at her, trying to hide his grief.

Now Julie was kneeling beside the bed, holding Aunt Puss's hands. She made no attempt to hide her tears. "Always, I've been mean to you, I've been mean and hateful to everyone," she sobbed, "and now you saved my life. Can you ever forgive me?" She buried her face in the feather pillow from which Aunt Puss was looking at her, still smiling. Julie's body was shaken by sobs.

"Honey, don't you think about it another minute." Aunt Puss's eyes were closed now and her voice was only a whisper but she was still smiling. "If you have been mean I done forgot it," she murmured. "Forgot it forevermore. An' Godamighty's forgot it too."

April still comes to Spurger and sunlight floods the countryside. White perch dart in and out the shady coves along the length of Beech Creek, and the mockingbird sings in the big elm tree outside Aunt Puss's kitchen window. But something is missing, something vital and vibrant is gone, something that will long be remembered in the little community of Spurger where once there lived a remarkable woman.

Aunt Puss

Aunt [101] *Puss*

PAISANO ADVISORY BOARD

JOHN Q. ANDERSON
The University of Houston

EDWIN W. GASTON, JR.
Stephen F. Austin State College

NORMAN L. McNEIL
Sul Ross State College

DESIGN : WILLIAM D. WITTLIFF